The Disequilibrium Model in a Controlled Economy

D0815433

The Disequilibrium Model in a Controlled Economy

David H. Howard
Federal Reserve Board

Lexington Books
D.C. Heath and Company
Lexington, Massachusetts
Toronto

Library of Congress Cataloging in Publication Data

Howard, David H.
    The disequilibrium model in a controlled economy.

    Bibliography: p.
    Includes index.
    1. Russia—Economic conditions—1965–
—Mathematical models. 2. Equilibrium (Economics)—
I. Title.
HC336.23.H68   330.9'47'085   78–24828
ISBN 0–669–02851–7

Published simultaneously in Canada.

Printed in the United States of America.

International Standard Book Number: 0–669–02851–7

Library of Congress Catalog Card Number: 78–24828

To my parents
Henry and Alice Howard

Contents

List of Figures and Tables

Figures

Tables

Acknowledgments

Some of the material in this book has appeared elsewhere. Parts of chapters 4 to 8 are taken from "The Disequilibrium Model in a Controlled Economy: An Empirical Test of the Barro-Grossman Model," *American Economic Review* 66 (December 1976); parts of chapters 4 and 8 are from "Rationing, Quantity Constraints, and Consumption Theory," *Econometrica* 45 (March 1977); and some of chapter 6 is taken from "A Note on Hidden Inflation in the Soviet Union," *Soviet Studies* 28 (October 1976). These are reprinted with permission.

I would like to thank the American Economic Association as well as Robert Barro and Herschel Grossman for permission to quote from Robert J. Barro and Herschel I. Grossman, "A General Disequilibrium Model of Income and Employment," *American Economic Review* 61 (March 1971).

Many people have helped me at various stages. I would like especially to thank the following people for their help: Richard Berner, Kenneth Clarkson, Herschel Grossman, Dale Henderson, Bennett McCallum, John Moore, Gertrude Schroeder, Roger Sherman, John Whitaker, anonymous referees for the *American Economic Review* and *Econometrica,* and George Borts of the *American Economic Review.*

I would like to thank the Thomas Jefferson Center Foundation of Charlottesville, Virginia, for its generous support of both my graduate studies and the research and writing of my book.

I would like also to thank Sandra Clayton and June Watkins for typing the manuscript.

This study represents my views solely and should not be interpreted as reflecting the views of the Board of Governors of the Federal Reserve System or other members of its staff.

The Disequilibrium Model in a Controlled Economy

1 Introduction

There has been a great deal of interest in disequilibrium theory in the economics literature.[1] This book applies the formal analysis of disequilibrium developed in the literature, with some extensions and modifications, to the study of a particular controlled economy: the Soviet Union.

The basic features of Soviet economic policy are well known. Briefly, there has been an emphasis on capital-goods production at the expense of consumer-goods production. The vehicle for transmitting this set of priorities to the economy is a centrally formulated plan legally binding on a primarily nationalized economy. "Campaigns" or crash programs to accomplish certain goals have been common, and in general plans have been ambitious; that is, plans have been "taut."[2] Coercion of labor has been common, sometimes as outright direction of labor, at other times in the form of constraints on mobility.

One particularly outstanding feature of the Soviet economy is the pervasiveness of disequilibria. Indeed, disequilibrium is an integral part of the Soviet system. Supply problems have plagued enterprises throughout Soviet history, and shortages of consumer goods have been a special problem. There are some alleged advantages of these disequilibria, in particular those arising from the use of campaigns. These involve the strategy of unbalanced growth, according to which the disequilibria result in "creative tensions" and act as "stimuli for further change."[3] Dodge and Wilber maintain that the disequilibria are an important and beneficial part of Soviet development strategy.[4] One of these disequilibria, consumer-good shortages, is the subject of this book.

There are three main objectives of this book. The first is to investigate theoretically the effects of disequilibrium on economic behavior. The second is to test empirically the disequilibrium model, using data from the Soviet Union. The third and most specific objective is to analyze a period of macroeconomic disequilibrium in the Soviet economy.

An important part of the analysis involves individual behavior under quantity constraints. Recent literature on disequilibrium is helpful for understanding such behavior. Chapter 2 presents a survey of the relevant literature on macroeconomic disequilibrium. Chapter 3 presents an elementary description of certain institutional arrangements in the Soviet economy. The general purpose of this chapter is to describe the economic environment of the private citizen in the Soviet economy during the period examined in this book.

Chapter 4 contains the theoretical model. It first analyzes individual household behavior when faced with quantity constraints, particularly with shortages

1

of consumer goods. The household maximizes utility subject to a budget constraint and a set of quantity constraints. It is shown that if two goods are substitutes and one is in excess demand, then the demand for the one not in excess demand changes in the opposite direction from a change in the quantity available of the one in excess demand. For the case of complements, the change is in the same direction. The signs of the various price effects and the real-balance effect are also determined. Next, the model is simplified so that only four goods are included in the household's utility function: leisure, a constrained consumption good, an unconstrained consumption good, and saving. From the results of the general case it follows that if all four goods are substitutes, then an increase (decrease) in the quantity of the constrained-consumption good leads to an increase (decrease) in labor supply and decreases (increases) in the demands for the unconstrained-consumption good and saving. Assuming no distribution effects, aggregate functions with properties similar to the individual ones are obtained. Then the remaining equations in the model are specified. Finally, the model is applied to the Soviet Union.

In chapter 5, the political economy of the disequilibrium model is discussed. The relation between the governmental determination of an economy's saving decision and labor freedom is investigated.

Chapter 6 discusses the data used and presents some estimates of price and consumption-goods volume indexes. Chapter 7 contains empirical tests, using three-stage least squares on annual data for the 1955–1967 period. It is discovered that the disequilibrium model performs well. Elasticities of response are calculated in order to obtain the household response pattern to repressed inflation. It is ascertained that for the household sector, saving is the most responsive outlet for repressed inflation in the Soviet Union, collective farm market demand is the next most responsive, and labor supply is the least.

In chapter 8 conclusions and implications are presented.

Notes

1. For example, Robert Clower, "The Keynesian Counterrevolution: A Theoretical Appraisal"; Axel Leijonhufvud, *On Keynesian Economics and the Economics of Keynes;* Robert J. Barro and Herschel I. Grossman, "A General Disequilibrium Model of Income and Employment."

2. Tautness as an economic policy is discussed in Herbert S. Levine, "Pressure and Planning in the Soviet Economy."

3. Alec Nove, *The Soviet Economy,* p. 327. Nove is paraphrasing the unbalanced-growth literature. Nove also points out the role played by campaigns in controlling bureaucrats' behavior (p. 329).

4. Norton T. Dodge and Charles K. Wilber, "The Relevance of Soviet Industrial Experience for Less Developed Economies," pp. 333–38.

2

The Development of the Disequilibrium Model

Central to the analysis of this book is the concept of an economy in disequilibrium and the influence of quantities on demand functions in such situations. The purpose of this chapter is to survey the major contributions in the modern economics literature to the understanding of these subjects. That is, this chapter surveys the development of the disequilibrium model. Many modern treatments are in terms of interpretations or reinterpretations of Keynes.[1] This means that this survey should start with Keynes. However, because it is not an objective of this book to write doctrinal history, the discussion of Keynes can be brief. Specifically, attention can be confined to *The General Theory of Employment, Interest, and Money* and its treatment of the aspects of disequilibrium which are relevant to the present analysis. A complete account of Keynes' theory is clearly beyond the scope of this book.

Keynes states that "the pure theory of what determines the *actual employment* of the available resources has seldom been examined in great detail."[2] Later in the book Keynes states that his objective is "to discover what determines [this] volume of employment."[3] Throughout the book Keynes makes it clear that this volume of actual employment can be less than full employment.[4] The major cause of this disequilibrium in the labor market is said to be insufficient effective aggregate demand, and the dynamics of the situation are studied mostly with the use of multiplier analysis.

A key tool in Keynes's analysis, which is essential in understanding Keynes's disequilibrium theory, is the consumption function. Keynes wants to relate consumption to the level of employment. He chooses income as a proxy for employment that is satisfactory in most cases. He then defines what he calls the "*propensity to consume* as the functional relationship χ between Y_w, a given level of income in terms of wage-units, and C_w, the expenditure on consumption out of that level of income, so that

$$C_w = \chi(Y_w) \quad \text{or} \quad C = W\chi(Y_w)."[5]$$

After discussing other influences on consumption, he concludes that "aggregate income . . . is, as a rule, the principal variable upon which the consumption-constituent of the aggregate demand function will depend."[6] Keynes himself claims that this relationship between aggregate income and consumption is "absolutely fundamental to the theory of effective demand as set forth in [*The General Theory of Employment, Interest, and Money*]".[7] But the theoretical

3

foundation of such a function is not clear. In a general equilibrium model, demands are functions solely of prices (and endowments), and labor supply (or labor income) is a choice variable rather than an argument in the demand functions. How, then, do the quantities (employment or income) enter Keynes's functions? This question and other disequilibrium topics are the subjects of the literature discussed later.

In *Money, Interest, and Prices,* Patinkin puts together a so-called Keynesian general equilibrium model of the economy.[8] However, in chapter 13 he addresses specifically the problem of involuntary unemployment, that is, disequilibrium.[9] Patinkin defines voluntary action to be when an economic unit is "on" an ordinary demand or supply curve; that is, an economic unit is acting voluntarily when its behavior can be described by such curves. Because it is only in general equilibrium that all demand and supply functions can be simultaneously satisfied, it follows that all economic units are acting voluntarily only in a state of general equilibrium. The only disequilibrium situation with which Patinkin is concerned is that of involuntary unemployment, that is, when workers are forced off their supply-of-labor curve. Involuntary unemployment is equal to excess supply of labor at the going wage rate.

In Patinkin's analysis, a downward shift in aggregate demand creates a deflationary gap. Firms must either cut output or accumulate inventories. Since the automatic adjustment-forces in this case are likely to be slow-working, the former option is taken, at least in cases of a major shift in aggregate demand. Thus there is involuntary unemployment. Even if the real wage should adjust, employment would be less than full general equilibrium employment. Later analysis explains why, given excess supply of labor, insufficient aggregate demand might persist.[10]

To Patinkin, then, the cause of unemployment is insufficient aggregate demand. More to the point of this book, he recognizes clearly how quantity constraints influence the demand for labor. He says,

> [An ordinary] demand function for labor describes the behavior of firms maximizing profits within a framework of perfect competition. This means that the planned labor input it specifies for any given real wage rate reflects the firm's assumptions *that they will be able to sell all of their resulting output at the prevailing market price.* Hence any development in the commodity market which invalidates this crucial assumption must also invalidate these plans.[11]

That is, current transactions or quantity constraints influence economic behavior. In his discussions Patinkin makes it clear that he recognizes the difference between actual and desired magnitudes and functions. At one point he virtually says that to describe market behavior the actual demand for labor and the notional supply are the relevant functions, a point made later by Clower with reference to commodity demand and labor supply.[12]

Patinkin calls his framework one of "dynamic disequilibrium" (as opposed to "static equilibrium analysis"). He claims that to study involuntary unemployment it is necessary to use such a framework. In fact, in his view "the essence of dynamic analysis is involuntariness: its domain consists only of positions *off* the demand or supply curves."[13] Dealing with such positions can be difficult, but a distinction between constrained and notional demands (to be discussed shortly) makes it possible to alleviate much of the difficulty.[14]

Clower objects to the (then) standard "Keynesian" interpretation of Keynes.[15] He contends that the very things to which Keynes objected continue to be a part of contemporary economic theory. In order to show this, Clower first presents traditional theory on an aggregate basis.

He considers a two-sector economy consisting of firms and households and two types of goods—commodities and factors. There are m commodities and $n - m$ factors. The firm supplies the former and demands the latter, and the household does the reverse. The symbols s_i, $i = 1, \ldots, m$, and d_j, $j = m + 1, \ldots, n$, denote the firm's planned supply and demand functions, and similarly s_j and d_i denote the household's. Note that i means a commodity and j a factor. Market prices are represented by $P_1, \ldots, P_{n-1}$ ($P_n \equiv 1$) or the vector $\mathbf{P}$. The firm's profit (r) maximization problem is to maximize

$$r = \sum_1^m P_i s_i - \sum_{m+1}^n P_j d_j$$

subject to its transformation function; from it, the (planned) supply and demand functions $\bar{s}_i$ (P) and $\bar{d}_j$ (P) can be obtained. Similarly, for the household, maximizing $U(d_1, \ldots, d_m; s_{m+1}, \ldots, s_n)$ subject to the budget constraint yields $\bar{d}_i$ (P,r) and $\bar{s}_j$ (P,r); profit r enters because of its presence in the budget constraint. When individual trading plans, as expressed by these functions, are consistent, that is, demand equals supply in each market, the economy is said to be in a state of equilibrium. If they are not consistent, some plans will be frustrated at prevailing prices. When plans are frustrated, prices are presumed to vary in order to equate supply and demand.

In Clower's view, this provides a theory of equilibrium but not of disequilibrium.[16] This, Clower contends, was also Keynes's view—orthodox economics is adequate for equilibrium but not for disequilibrium analysis.

Based on textual evidence plus the maintained assumption that Keynes had something important to say and that he did so in a competent manner, Clower contends that an important part of Keynes's indictment of orthodox theory is based on an "attack on the orthodox theory of household behavior." Clower further argues that Keynes used a "more general theory" in which demand functions "include quantities as well as prices as independent variables. . . ."[17] For present purposes it does not matter if Clower's interpretation of Keynes is correct. However, this "more general theory" of household behavior is used here in order to analyze the effects of quantity constraints on household behavior.

Clower points out that quantity variables do not appear in the demand and supply functions of a general equilibrium model (a point which raises questions as to the derivation of Keynes's consumption function); but when the prevailing price vector is not an equilibrium one, the problem of the influence of transactions (that is, a quantity) at nonequilibrium prices on demand and supply functions must be faced. This problem is usually solved by means of a recontracting arrangement or by assuming that disequilibrium transactions can be ignored. Clower asks the question of what happens when these two assumptions cannot be made, which is, presumably, often. He next defines disequilibrium transaction quantities by supposing, quite reasonably, that actual transactions equal the minimum of planned supply and demand.[18] This book uses this definition also.

Orthodox theory does not distinguish between planned and realized magnitudes as Clower's formulation does because in the context of that theory the distinction is not meaningful since disequilibrium states are not permitted (except only as transitory phenomena in which no transactions take place). However, Clower points out that if disequilibrium states are permitted, "the distinction between plans and realizations becomes both meaningful and theoretically relevant."[19] Clower's dichotomy between realized or actual magnitudes and planned or notional magnitudes is of utmost importance to his analysis. For the individual household, actual purchases must equal actual receipts. Clower contrasts this with what he calls "Say's Principle" which is a rational planning postulate that planned purchases equal planned receipts. Maximizing utility subject to a budget constraint expressed in terms of planned purchases and receipts allows derivation of notional household demand and supply functions $\bar{d}_i$ (P,r) and $\bar{s}_j$ (P,r). But these notional functions cannot necessarily be used to represent market demand and supply because to do so one must assume that "every household expects to be able to buy or sell any desired quantity of each and every commodity at prevailing market prices." Orthodox analysis assumes that plans to sell, buy, and save are carried out simultaneously. However this requires that the economy always be in equilibrium since "not every household can buy and sell just what it pleases if supply exceeds demand somewhere in the economy."[20]

Clower calls this view of household decision making the "unified decision" hypothesis. For the analysis of disequilibrium Clower proposes instead his "dual decision hypothesis." He contends that if an individual is involuntarily unemployed, he will curtail, at least to an extent, his current consumption plans. He then concludes that the usual demand functions are irrelevant since the realized-income constraint will reduce actual consumption below the level predicted by orthodox analysis.[21]

Formally, orthodox theory has the household maximizing $U(d_1, \ldots, d_m; s_{m+1}, \ldots, s_n)$ subject to

$$\sum_{1}^{m} P_i d_i - \sum_{m+1}^{n} P_j s_j - r = 0$$

from which are derived $\bar{d}_i \, (P,r)$ and $\bar{s}_j \, (P,r)$ (as mentioned above) as long as

$$\sum_{m+1}^{n} P_j s_j^0 \geqslant \sum_{m+1}^{n} P_j \bar{s}_j$$

(the zero superscript indicates a realized magnitude) that is, as long as realized income is not less than notional income. If, however,

$$\sum_{m+1}^{n} P_j s_j^0 < \sum_{m+1}^{n} P_j \bar{s}_j$$

then a second round of decisions is required. The problem then becomes to maximize the same $U \, (\cdot)$ subject to the new constraint

$$\sum_{1}^{m} P_i d_i - \sum_{m+1}^{n} P_j s_j^0 - r = 0$$

Solving this yields a set of "constrained" demand functions

$$\hat{d}_i(P, \sum_{m+1}^{n} P_j s_j^0 + r) \equiv \hat{d}_i(P,Y)$$

Thus Clower postulates a two-step process in which notional supply is first determined and then constrained demand (given current income). Therefore except where realized income equals notional income, $d_i(P,Y)$ and $\bar{s}_j(P,r)$ rather than $\bar{d}_i(P,r)$ and $\bar{s}_j(P,r)$ "are the relevant providers of market signals."[22]

Clower concludes that this hypothesis recognizes that realized income can impose a restriction on effective demand.[23] However, the hypothesis is much more powerful than that. Clower's analysis, supplemented by Patinkin's analysis and properly generalized, shows the implications of any quantity constraint on household behavior on all markets. This generalization is done by Barro and Grossman.

Of Leijonhufvud's book on Keynes's economics, only chapter 2 is of direct relevance to this book.[24] In this chapter he further develops the analysis put forth in Clower's 1965 paper which has just been discussed. Leijonhufvud confines himself to deflationary situations and analyzes "the nature of the disequilibrium situation at some point within the time-interval before the economy settles on a new equilibrium time-path."[25]

According to Leijonhufvud, Keynes was mostly interested in the economy's adjustment process in situations of disequilibrium. Following Clower, he points out the distinctive feature of Keynesian supply and demand equations—the presence of quantity variables as arguments. This is because for Keynes the adjustment process consists primarily of quantity changes whereas Marshallian adjustment is by price movements. In Marshallian analysis prices adjust in the short run with output adjustment taking place later. Leijonhufvud states:

> *In the Keynesian macrosystem the Marshallian ranking of price- and quantity-adjustment speeds is reversed:* In the shortest period flow quantities are freely variable, but one or more prices are given, and the admissible range of variation for the rest of the prices is thereby limited.[26]

If this is so, Leijonhufvud contends, then "false trading" is inevitable; that is, transactions will take place at disequilibrium prices. The usual procedure is to assume away this problem. As has been seen, Clower addresses himself to the situation where it cannot be assumed away. At false prices some notional transactions do not take place (Clower's notional/constrained dichotomy), and this affects aggregate demand (and supply in inflationary situations). That is, realized quantities enter the demand functions as independent variables. This, of course, is the familiar Keynesian consumption function. There can be "multiplier" effects; an initial fall in aggregate demand produces, in the absence of instant price and wage adjustment, an excess supply of labor, which leads to a further drop in effective aggregate demand, and so on.

As can be seen, a key point in Leijonhufvud's interpretation of Keynes is that price adjustment is not instantaneous. Here the essence of Leijonhufvud's analysis is that the Walrasian auctioneer does not exist; transactors do not have perfect knowledge. Without this information the equilibrium price vector is unknown, and so prices bid and asked must proceed more cautiously. Since the knowledge needed cannot be supplied by a "mechanism *unrelated* to the trading process itself,"[27] false trading will take place and this will further complicate the search for the equilibrium price vector (for example, set in motion the "multiplier" process). Leijonhufvud contrasts the Walrasian model's provision of costless price information with Clower's dual-decision hypothesis where households are instead informed about quantities that they can sell prior to planning purchases. Relying primarily on the analysis of Alchian,[28] Leijonhufvud shows why prices can be expected to be rigid or "sticky" in a world where information is costly. An individual or firm facing a decline in demand for its services or product must change its asking price to the new market-clearing level. This level, however, is unknown. Thus, the individual or firm must search the market in order to ascertain it. While search continues, the reservation price is set and reset according to the newly acquired information. Initially the only information that the individual or firm has to go on is the price prevailing prior to the change in demand. Hence until better information is generated, the price is rigid.

Next Leijonhufvud discusses Clower's distinction between notional and effective functions. He points out, without much elaboration, that this analysis applies to inflationary situations also. Clower's point that notional supply and constrained or effective demand functions provide the relevant market signals in a deflationary situation is made clear in Leijonhufvud's account of the "income-constrained process." He says that following the initial shift in demand,

> transactors with unemployed resources . . . will generally reduce their expenditures in other markets. *Effective demands* are thus reduced also in markets on which the initial disturbance may have had no impact. Unemployed resources emerge in these markets also and *the search instituted by unemployed workers and producers* with excess capacity will yield information on "effective" demands, not on "notional" demands. The "multiplier" repercussions thus set in motion make the information acquired "dated" even while it is being gathered.[29]

Thus, the initial shock is amplified. Because money is used as the means of payment, wage bargains are in monetary, not real, terms. Hence the workers have no way of communicating their notional demand for commodities to the producers. They demand money rather than commodities during the bargaining process. Only after getting this money wage can they effectively communicate their demand for commodities. However, in the absence of such a demand, the producers will not hire more workers, so both sides are frustrated with excess supply.

In his 1969 article, Grossman discusses disequilibrium situations in terms of "spillover effects." These arise, he says, when it is assumed that an individual's actions in a particular market "depend upon the transactions which he actually executes in other markets."[30] He goes on to state that spillover effects would appear to be both a "fundamental implication of maximizing behaviour" and an "essential characteristic for a model of markets without recontracting."[31]

In a 1971 paper, Grossman presents "effective" demand functions that are related to all notional demands in the system.[32] Grossman's "generalized" dual-decision hypothesis consists of bringing the effects of constraints on all markets into the decision process.[33] The decisionmaker looks at all perceived constraints before deciding on all his effective demands.

Grossman writes equations reflecting the spillover effects of other excess demands, for example,

$$b'_i = b_i + \alpha_i \left(y_i - y'_i + f_i y'_i \right)$$

where b_i and y_i are the ith individual's notional demands for b and y, the prime indicates effective demand, α_i is a functional relationship involving the parameters, $y_i - y'_i + f_i y'_i$ is i's actual unfulfilled excess demand for y, and f_i reflects i's queue position.[34] Grossman points out that effective demands "might be denoted as 'fixed-price-equilibrium' quantities, in the sense that they would have no tendency to change" as long as prices and the rate of interest did not change.[35] This type of approach is used when the concept of a stationary disequilibrium state is developed in chapter 4.

In their 1971 paper, Barro and Grossman state that "Keynesian theory proposes as a general case a system of markets which are not always cleared." This implies that actual transaction quantities can diverge from the quantities that individuals supply or demand. "Thus, the natural focus of Keynesian analysis is on the implications for behavior in one market of the existence of such a divergence in another market."[36] Barro and Grossman's analysis is aimed at studying such disequilibrium phenomena.

Their analytical framework consists of three goods—labor services, consumption goods, and money—and two economic agents—the firm and the household. The former maximizes profit, and the latter maximizes utility. The model's variables are defined as follows: y is the quantity of commodities, x is the quantity of labor services, m is the increase in real money balances, π is the amount of real profits, M is the initial stock of nominal money balances, P is the money price of commodities, and w is the real wage rate. Their analysis takes a price and wage vector as given and works out the implied income and employment levels.

Barro and Grossman summarize and express the analyses of Patinkin and Clower as follows. Let y^S = notional supply of consumer goods, y = actual (realized) sales, and $x^{D'}$ = effective demand for labor (the superscript convention holds throughout). Then if $y < y^S$, profit maximization implies simply the selection of minimum x to produce the given y. If $\pi = y - wx^{D'}$ subject to $y = F(x)$ with y given, then $x^{D'} = F^{-1}(y)$; and since $y < y^S$, this implies $x^{D'} < x^D$. (This is Patinkin's result that insufficient commodity demand leads to unemployment.) Under equilibrium conditions the household can sell or buy as much of any good as it wants at the going price. The utility function is assumed to be $U(x^S, y^D, M/P + m^D)$, and the budget constraint is $\pi + wx^S = y^D + m^D$. Maximization of utility implies notional functions x^S, y^D, and m^D as functions of w, M/P, and π. However, when labor is in excess supply, the household cannot sell its notional labor supply or earn its notional income wx^S. Labor income becomes exogenous in the maximization problem. Thus $x < x^S$ and the household maximizes $U(x, y^{D'}, M/P + m^{D'})$ subject to $\pi + wx = y^{D'} + m^{D'}$. This implies

$y^{D'} = y^{D'} (\pi + wx, M/P)$, and $m^{D'} = m^{D'} (\pi + wx, M/P)$. Since $x < x^S$, this implies, in normal cases, $y^{D'} < y^D$ and $m^{D'} < m^D$. (This includes Clower's point that unemployment leads to excess supply on the commodity market.) Barro and Grossman point out that the above demand equations

> have the form of the usual Keynesian consumption and saving functions. Labor income enters the consumption and saving functions as it represents the constraint upon the demand for current output imposed by the excess supply of labor.[37]

It is further pointed out that the Patinkin and Clower analyses are formally analogous, involving profit and utility maximization, respectively, under conditions of quantity constraints, and that they are complementary in that each is needed to close the other system. Barro and Grossman then take this closed system, that is, where both output demand and labor demand are explained, and use it to analyze the case of general disequilibrium involving excess supply and the case involving excess demand. For the purposes of this book attention can be confined to the latter case.

With excess demand for labor, the representative firm's effective supply of commodities is less than its notional supply because of the constraint on available labor. For present purposes, however, the more interesting question has to do with household behavior. The representative household is only able to obtain y amount of commodities, $y < y^D$. It then must choose among saving its excess purchasing power, reducing its supply of labor, or some combination of the two.[38] Barro and Grossman derive effective supply and demand functions. That is, the household maximizes $U(x^{S'}, y, M/P + m^{D'})$ subject to $\pi + wx^{S'} = y + m^{D'}$. Utility maximization implies an effective supply of labor of the form $x^{S'} = x^{S'}(w, M/P, \pi, y)$ and an effective demand for saving $m^{D'} = m^{D'}(w, M/P, \pi, y)$. Note the existence of y, constrained consumption or the quantity of consumer goods available, in these equations. The authors assert that $\delta x^{S'}/\delta y > 0$ and $\delta m^{D'}/\delta y < 0$. They point out that the reduction-in-labor-supply response to frustrated consumption "probably becomes more important when excess commodity demand is chronic, as in wartime or during other periods of rationing and price controls." In a footnote they refer to the applicability of this to the Soviet Union. They go on to state:

> however, given that consumption, saving, and leisure in aggregate are substitutes, in general some combination of the two options will always be optimal. Excess demand will generally result in some fall of output.
>
> Classical analysis, in which labor supply is solely a function of the real wage, assumes that households channel all frustrated commodity demand into forced saving. The possibility of reduced labor supply is ignored. However, the inclusion of this option is especially interesting,

since it has the apparently paradoxical implication that excess commodity demand can result in decreased employment and output.[39]

This implication is of great importance in the analysis of the Soviet economy.

By means of a diagram, Barro and Grossman stress that an excessively low real wage is not necessary for excess demand for labor and that "with commodities in excess demand, the quantity of employment will generally be below the full employment level."[40] The diagram depicts the demand for labor as a decreasing function of the real wage, the notional supply of labor as an increasing function of the real wage, and an effective supply of labor (when $y < y^D$) which is to the left of the notional supply curve in the relevant range. In this diagram, there is excess demand even if the wage equals that necessary to clear the notional labor market, that is, even if it is not too low. The second point is more interesting from the point of view of this book. Since the amount exchanged on a market is determined by the short side of the market, employment can be no greater than the amount supplied in this case (because constrained consumption puts the household on its effective supply of labor schedule $x^{S'}$). Even if the wage rises to a level consistent with labor market clearing, and therefore excess demand for labor is eliminated, the conclusion holds. That is, employment is still below the full employment level. Since, as mentioned, $x^{S'}$ determines actual employment, there will necessarily be a gap because $x^{S'}$ lies to the left of the notional supply-of-labor curve at each wage rate in the relevant range. "Full employment," in case it is not clear, refers to that level of employment consistent with general equilibrium, that is, equilibrium in all markets. It has to do, therefore, with notional supplies and demands.

The Barro and Grossman article is an extremely important one. It combines the analyses of Patinkin and Clower into one consistent, self-contained, and generalized model of an economy under conditions of disequilibrium. It generates the Patinkin and Clower results as well as some original ones. Most important for present purposes is their analysis of the case of general disequilibrium with excess demand. Here the conclusion of interest to this book is that with constrained consumption the household saves more money and supplies less labor. That is, employment and therefore output fall in response to an insufficient supply of consumer goods.[41]

This chapter has briefly traced the evolution of modern disequilibrium theory. One sees that an important part of the disequilibrium model is that quantities or current transactions enter into the system's demand functions; that is, the functions include quantity variables as well as prices and endowments. Quantity constraints lead to constrained functions, which in turn can have further repercussions on the economy, serving to amplify the original shock to the system or at least delaying the adjustment process.

Notes

1. Two major contributors to the literature on disequilibrium maintain that Keynes was the initiator of modern disequilibrium analysis. See Robert Clower, "The Keynesian Counterrevolution," and Axel Leijonhufvud, *On Keynesian Economics and the Economics of Keynes.* Other analysts maintain that he was not; see Herschel I. Grossman, "Was Keynes a 'Keynesian'? A Review Article," and Leland B. Yeager, "The Keynesian Diversion." This question is not a concern of this book.

2. John Maynard Keynes, *The General Theory of Employment, Interest, and Money,* p. 4.

3. Ibid., p. 89.

4. See, for example, Keynes, ibid., p. 30.

5. Ibid., p. 90.

6. Ibid., p. 96.

7. Keynes, "The General Theory of Employment," pp. 219-20.

8. Don Patinkin, *Money, Interest, and Prices.* See Donald P. Tucker, "Patinkin's Macro Model as a Model of Market Disequilibrium." In this interesting article Tucker criticizes Patinkin's model and revises it so that it can cope with disequilibria other than unemployment. He does this by incorporating excess demands into Patinkin's equations. This can lead to econometric difficulties as is discussed in Tucker, "Macroeconomic Models and the Demand for Money under Market Disequilibrium." Tucker's purpose is to take into account the effects of quantity constraints on the economy. This is what is done in chapter 4.

9. In *Money, Interest, and Prices,* pp. 337-38, Patinkin states that "Keynesian economics is the economics of unemployment *dis*equilibrium." Clower, in "Keynes and the Classics: A Dynamical Perspective," p. 322, also takes this view in such statements as "Keynes dealt with disequilibrium states" and "Keynesian theory is mainly concerned with disequilibrium states."

10. See the discussions of Clower and Robert J. Barro and Grossman below.

11. Patinkin, *Money, Interest, and Prices,* p. 319.

12. Ibid., p. 321. For a discussion of Clower and references, see below.

13. Ibid., p. 323.

14. In a 1949 article, Patinkin formulated much of the analysis of chapter 13: "Involuntary Unemployment and the Keynesian Supply Function."

15. Clower, "The Keynesian Counterrevolution."

16. Ibid., pp. 107-8.

17. Ibid., p. 111.

18. Ibid., p. 113.

19. Ibid., p. 116.

20. Ibid., p. 117.

21. Ibid., p. 118. As Tucker, "Macroeconomic Models," p. 63, points out, expected constraints (for example, anticipated income) can also influence this decision process.

22. Clower, "The Keynesian Counterrevolution," p. 119.

23. Clower contends that Keynesian economics assumes that demand is a function of current market transactions while orthodox economics assumes that demand is independent of such transactions. Ibid., pp. 123-24.

24. Leijonhufvud, *On Keynesian Economics.*

25. Ibid., p. 50.

26. Ibid., p. 52.

27. Ibid., p. 69.

28. Armen A. Alchian, "Information Costs, Pricing, and Resource Unemployment." In *Keynes and the Classics,* p. 31, Leijonhufvud credits W.H. Hutt with originally developing this analysis.

29. Leijonhufvud, *On Keynesian Economics,* pp. 84-85.

30. Grossman, "Theories of Markets without Recontracting," p. 477.

31. Ibid., p. 478.

32. Grossman, "Money, Interest, and Prices in Market Disequilibrium," p. 945.

33. Ibid., p. 951.

34. Ibid., p. 955.

35. Ibid., p. 958.

36. Barro and Grossman, "A General Disequilibrium Model of Income and Employment," p. 82.

37. Ibid., p. 88.

38. This choice is discussed in the rationing and price control literature. See, for example, James Tobin, "A Survey of the Theory of Rationing."

39. Barro and Grossman, "A General Disequilibrium Model," p. 91. This last "apparently paradoxical" implication is also discussed in Barro and Grossman, "Suppressed Inflation and the Supply Multiplier."

40. Barro and Grossman, "A General Disequilibrium Model," p. 91. The diagram is figure 6 on p. 92.

41. Barro and Grossman, *Money, Employment and Inflation,* further develops and consolidates the analysis in their articles, but for present purposes their 1971 model is relevant.

3 Institutional Framework

This chapter outlines the environment of the Soviet household during the 1955–1967 period (roughly), in order to make the subsequent chapters more understandable. This chapter does not provide a detailed description or analysis of the Soviet institutional framework. The reader is referred to the sources cited in the footnotes in this chapter for that purpose.

The Labor Market

The first question that arises involves the extent to which the Soviet labor market was a free market during the 1955–1967 period. Although most observers agree that it was to a large extent free, various laws and attempts at planning kept the worker from being completely free. For example, the worker could choose his job, but he was more or less compelled to have a job or be temporarily between jobs. The constraints imposed by the government on labor supply merit examination.

In her book on Soviet trade unions, Brown states that "the long history of regimentation of labor, coercion, terror, the secret police, the labor camps, under Stalin, still leaves its mark on industrial relations."[1] One such mark is the use of such things as "antiparasite" laws to enforce the Soviet ideology that every citizen has a duty to work. This ideology is probably the most important institution in the labor market. It was written into the Soviet constitution in article 12: "Work in the U.S.S.R. is a duty and a matter of honor for every able-bodied citizen, in accordance with the principle: 'he who does not work, neither shall he eat'"[2] This is reinforced from time to time with such things as the 1970 joint directive of the central committee of the communist party and the council of ministers, "On Measures for the Strengthening of the Struggle with Persons Who Shun Socially Useful Work and Lead Anti-Societal Parasitical Ways of Life."[3] There were economic and criminal penalties for this and similar crimes.

Under Stalin, the laws prohibited workers from quitting without permission, but workers could be transferred involuntarily and severe penalties were given for "truancy." According to Brown, "The use of coercion declined in the early 1950's, until, with the complete repeal of the 1940 laws on April 25, 1956, freedom of choice of jobs again came to the fore. Workers could then leave jobs on two weeks' notice."[4] Schroeder agrees with this observation concerning the decline in coercion and states that "the repeal of the punitive measures in 1956 merely legitimized the existing situation."[5] However, there may have been a one-time increase in labor turnover in 1956 because of the repeal of the laws.

Thus during the present period of study the Soviet worker could change jobs without fear of legal consequences. However, the length of time between jobs and the number of changes in one year were subject to government scrutiny and control. Examples of government coercion in these areas are provisions for disciplinary action against "rolling stones" (those who quit more than once in one year) and laws providing for reduced benefits for those who spent more than thirty days between jobs. Antiparasite laws have the same general effect of reducing frequency and duration of labor turnover. Labor mobility was further hampered by the shortage of housing.

Government control, or at least surveillance, of the work force was facilitated by the passport and workbook system. The passport is an identification document which must be carried by all adults who live in urban and some other specified areas. The workbook also contains identification along with a record of the worker's education, training, and job experience including reasons for past separations. The worker had to have these documents, and they had to be submitted when applying for a new job. No one could be hired without submitting his passport and workbook.

There were also some constraints on the demand for labor. In the Soviet Union it is illegal for a "private citizen to employ anyone to produce a commodity for sale."[6] Hence the demand for labor came largely from the state and cooperative sector. Schroeder points out that while a great deal of effort was devoted to planning labor demand, the plans rarely worked out. This is because enterprise managers were also subject to the output plan, which had a higher priority. In order to fulfill the latter, it was often necessary to violate the former. In addition, some excess (that is, above-plan) workers acted as insurance for the enterprise in its attempt to fulfill the output plan.

In competing for the services of labor, Soviet enterprises relied heavily on the use of money wages.[7] The wages acted as signals to the workers, and the level of wages and wage differentials influenced the decisions of both workers and managers. Wages and piece rates would appear to have been centrally set, but actually they were not. Because labor was mobile, the enterprises had to bid for their services. The result was upward pressure on money wages, and "overexpenditures of the planned wage funds in individual enterprises" were frequent.[8] Since expenditures were greater than planned, the balance between money income and the nominal value of goods and services available to the consumer tended to become upset. The Soviet worker's mobility foiled official plans and led to an inflationary tendency in the economy. Fearn describes this process very well. Competition among employers for workers led to upward pressures on money wages. Despite formal controls, the enterprises found it quite easy to obtain funds to finance these above-plan expenditures on wages. These overexpenditures resulted in an increase in the money supply unmatched by an increase in consumer-goods production; hence inflationary pressures resulted.[9] In the absence of flexible prices these pressures took the form of shortages and hoarding.

Many observers of the Soviet Union have commented on the emergence of labor shortages over the last two decades. As Feshbach and Rapawy make clear, these "shortages" have to do with labor supply relative to plans and especially relative to labor needed to achieve historic rates of growth of employment.[10] Without such increases in labor input other means of increasing output must be found. No doubt this is the reason that such labor shortages are a source of concern to Soviet planners. (This kind of shortage is compatible with a market-clearing wage and is not the same as the kind of shortage which is discussed in the analytical parts of this book, where a shortage is defined as excess demand at the prevailing market price.) Nove states that "the period of labour abundance is drawing to a close."[11] Indeed, by 1973 it had probably already drawn to a close. As Feshbach and Rapawy put it,

> In sum, there probably is an overall labor shortage in the Soviet Union as well as shortages in terms of geographic location, skills, and sectoral distribution. . . .
>
> Soviet planners are clearly concerned about the labor supply, and the thrust of all recent actions in the manpower field has been to ease a taut labor market.[12]

Labor supply shortages seem to have become a problem as early as 1959.[13]

Another labor market problem facing the Soviet authorities was that of labor turnover. This also indicates that there was a tight labor market in the Soviet Union. Western observers differ in their opinions about the seriousness of the situation. However, the Soviet authorities considered it a problem and took steps to combat it (for example, bonuses for long service and disciplinary action against "rolling stones", "parasites," and so on.) Evidence for the Soviet leadership's concern with turnover is presented in Miller's account of Khrushchev's speech of 1964 in which he denounced "flyers," "idlers," and "parasites" and equated a "good" worker with one who does not change jobs.[14]

Labor turnover could be either the cause or the effect of the tight labor market in the Soviet Union. To the extent that turnover is a reaction to wage competition, it is an effect of a tight labor market. To the extent that it is a form of a decrease in labor supply, it is a cause.

The Official Retail Market

The official retail market during the 1955-1967 period was composed of the state and consumer-cooperative retail networks. The former was predominantly urban, the latter rural. These networks amounted to 96 percent of all retail trade in 1965 and 1966.[15] The state network had both specialized stores and general department stores. The village shop was similar to a small general store, while larger population centers had larger stores. The consumer cooperatives were closely controlled by the state, and are not to be confused with Western cooperatives. In fact, as Nove points out, cooperative trade was ". . . to all intents and purposes . . . a branch of state trade. . . ."[16] In summarizing his description of Soviet state and cooperative trade, Goldman says that "all marketing activity is an extension of government activity" and that "there appears to be little competition between the major Soviet trade networks."[17] Finally, Goldman points out that service and convenience had been sacrificed in the official retail market.[18]

Hanson states that the Soviet consumer sector was technologically and organizationally weak compared to the rest of the economy and was short on capital.[19] Because the retail network was "relatively sparse," transactions costs to the consumer were increased since he had "to go further to shop than he would [have] in many other countries and [had] to select and buy goods in more crowded conditions." Hanson goes on to point out the large amount of time spent shopping by the Soviet consumer.[20]

Although there has been no formal rationing in the Soviet Union since 1947, there was excess demand on the official retail network throughout the present period of study. During the two decades since Stalin's death, the Soviet retail market shifted from one with excess demand for virtually all goods to one with excess demand for certain individual goods. By the late 1960s, in general, soft goods were no longer in excess demand, but consumer durables, quality food, and services such as housing were. As Bronson and Severin state, "The seller's market characteristic of the Stalin era, when extreme conditions of scarcity assured a ready market for whatever goods were available, has given way to a buyer's market for many products."[21] The seller's market continued into the early 1960s.[22] Hanson states that by the mid-1960s there were still shortages,[23] and (in 1968) he says that "there are a number of goods for which supply falls well short of effective demand at existing prices."[24] It seems that waiting lists were used for durable goods at least until the late 1960s or early 1970s.[25] The existence of waiting lists and queues throughout 1955–1967 is evidence of the excess demand on the official retail market during that period.[26] Excess demand has been a chronic problem in the Soviet Union. In the early 1970s, although not all goods were in excess demand, there were still "pervasive shortages of desired goods and services . . . and . . . continuing repressed inflation."[27]

The excess demand persisted because of institutional arrangements in the official retail market. Both supplies and prices on this market were set by the government. Since the government did not act like a profit-maximizing firm, neither output nor prices were necessarily adjusted to eliminate completely this excess demand.

The quantities of consumer goods available in the state and cooperative retail networks during the 1955–1967 period can be regarded as a state policy parameter; production and allocation of these goods were subject to the planning process. Quality and assortment of the goods sold were a problem on the official retail market. Although the authorities made an effort to give the consumers the assortment of goods that they wanted, this response was only casually related, if at all, to market forces. As Hanson puts it, "The ways in which the outputs of Soviet consumer goods are adapted to changes in the pattern of demand are, in Western eyes, rather devious, highly 'institutional,' unautomatic and of late frequently changed."[28] Nevertheless, as cumbersome as the adjustment process was, it worked after a fashion. However, it should be made clear that the adjustments discussed here have to do with output mix and not total output of consumer goods. As Hanson puts it, "The actual choice of rates of consumption and non-consumption in the Soviet Union is political, and seems likely to remain so."[29] The market influence on this is negligible. Thus, treating the supply of goods sold through the official retail market as a policy variable, rather than as the outcome of market forces, is acceptable on a global level and acceptable as an approximation on the level of individual goods as well.

The prices on the state and cooperative retail market during the present period of study can also be regarded as a policy parameter since they were set centrally and were only weakly realted to supply and demand (as is seen later). Some of these prices were uniform for the entire U.S.S.R., and some were differentiated by regions. Prices could be manipulated in an effort to equate supply and demand by means of changes in the turnover tax. As Nove points out, such a tax acts to isolate the supplier from the consumer and inhibits any change in quantity supplied in response to the changed retail price.[30]

If the authorities attempted to equate supply and demand, can it be said that prices were actually determined in the market? It is clear that market influences were at work; market information was one input into the decision process of the authorities. However, prices should still be considered a policy parameter, as Nove's discussion of retail prices makes clear. He says that prices were fixed to clear markets, except where social or political considerations took procedence. He continues that the prices were often set too low and that for some goods, especially durables, prices were deliberately set too low even though durables were scarce. The fact that prices of meat and dairy products were set too low is "only the most striking example of the impact of political considerations on retail prices."[31] Indeed, the mere fact that most prices were set centrally would seem to mean that they would be a policy parameter and not the outcome of market interaction. The administrators almost necessarily had a lack of knowledge about what exactly was a market-clearing price for the vast number of goods involved. When there was an imbalance, waiting lists or queues were resorted to (or inventories piled up); and the decision to vary price (usually by changing the turnover tax) might or might not have been made depending on other considerations, and in any case it was certainly not made instantaneously. As Nove points out, "There is a reluctance to make frequent changes in retail prices, and such changes are treated as a political matter, for the top leadership to decide."[32] Thus official retail prices were policy variables.

As has been seen, the government decided quantities and prices on the official retail market. However, it relied on the market to decide who got the goods; that is, there was free consumer choice. The consumer was by no means sovereign, but he was free to choose what he wanted to buy of the goods available.

The authorities attempted to achieve a balance of supply and demand on two different levels. First, they tried to balance personal money income with the nominal value of the goods and services available. Second, they usually tried to set a price which would equate supply and demand for each good. However, they were unsuccessful, in general, on both levels. (Earlier in this chapter the role of wage overexpenditures in upsetting the first balance is discussed.) Hanson states that in Soviet practice "there is certainly a tendency away from the imposition on consumers of an assortment and price structure such that markets in consumer goods remain out of balance."[33] Nevertheless, disequilibria (especially shortages) were the rule, largely because of centralized price fixing. Lack of information and changing conditions precluded market-clearing prices. Furthermore, to the extent that price changing was costly, some amount of disequilibrium was economically rational. Also, noneconomic criteria, as discussed earlier, often led to deliberate imbalances. In addition to the disequilibria in individual markets, there probably was general excess demand as well. (This question is examined in more detail in chapter 7.) Under Stalin, consumer-goods production and distribution were given low priority, and nearly everything was in excess demand. Subsequent leaders increased production of certain goods so that eventually many consumer goods were no longer in excess demand, but there still remained a great deal of excess demand concentrated on certain individual goods, for example, automobiles, and on higher-quality goods.[34]

The Collective Farm Market

During the 1955–1967 period, the collective farm market was the only organized free market in the Soviet Union. Both food items and handicrafts were sold on this market, but food was more important in terms of sales volume. There were many collective farm markets, both urban and rural. They were usually located in places with a large population flow. The markets were administered by local government authorities who oversaw operations, provided overhead (for example, stalls), advertised, taxed, and so on. Although the collective farm market's share of total food sales were small, it was extremely important because of the quality and availability of the products sold and because its share of sales of some types of food was large.

Both the collective farm and the individual peasant sold goods on the collective farm market. The farm, if it had a surplus after sales to the state, decided whether to sell on the free market depending on relative prices. Generally speaking, each household on a collective farm was allotted a personal plot of land that it could cultivate for its own use. The plots varied in size depending on local conditions. Households could also own chickens and a limited amount of livestock, which could be pastured on collective farmland. State farm workers and other employees could also hold personal plots. Produce from these private holdings was either consumed by the household or sold on the collective farm market. Until 1958 the peasants had to sell some of their produce to the state.

The prices on the collective farm market were determined by supply and demand. The government had "no direct control over prices" on this market.[35] In general, prices were higher on the free market than in the official retail market. There are at least two reasons for this. First, the official prices typically were set below market-clearing levels; second, the collective farm market goods were of better quality. Because the collective farm markets were localized, each market reflected local supply and demand conditions, and hence prices were not uniform throughout the Soviet Union.

As is the case in most economic activities in the Soviet Union, the government imposed various constraints (for example, size of plot) on the collective farm market as well. Official policy can affect the supply side of this market a great deal, for example, by varying taxes on or acreage allowed for the private plots or policies toward providing inputs such as hay and pasturing. Throughout Soviet history, including the period of this study, the authorities have alternated between a policy of relative encouragement and discouragement of private agricultural production.[36] In addition, of course, any policy change affecting the relative return between private and collective activity, notably changes in state procurement prices and the peasant pay system, would influence the supply on the collective farm market originating from individual peasants.

Despite the collective farm market's importance, the authorities' official policy opposed the institution. Although pragmatically it was allowed to continue, under restrictions, official policy stated that the private plot system was ideologically wrong and even that it inhibited production.[37] Ultimately the collective farm market is supposed to wither away as the state and cooperative sector comes to supply all needs.[38]

The Savings Bank System

The government controlled the savings banks, of which about three-quarters were cashiers' windows in post offices. There were different types of savings accounts, including both time and demand deposits. These deposits bear interest; during the period of study demand deposits paid 2 percent and time deposits 3 percent. The savings bank system handled "virtually all accounts . . . of individuals."[39] The savings banks bought state bonds with the money deposited in them.

The Soviet population had a few alternatives to savings accounts, including cash balances, government bonds, and investment in private housing. Unfortunately there are virtually no data on currency in circulation for the period studied, so the extent of hoarding cannot be estimated. However, Bronson and Severin state that "there is no evidence that deposits are increasing as a share of total savings," that is, as a share of savings accounts plus cash balances.[40] Voluntary state bonds were available throughout the period of this study (the interest rate was 3 percent). Compulsory bond purchases, abolished in 1957, amounted to taxes and are not considered here as an alternative. According to Miller, the private housing sector was fairly important; both enterprises and individuals built housing. Officially, private rents were not allowed, but this was disregarded in practice.[41]

Households used savings deposits for three major reasons. First, saving was a reaction to shortages of consumer goods, an outlet for purchasing power that could not be spent right away. Second, it was a means of storing up the funds necessary to purchase consumer durables and other goods involving a high price. Third, savings deposits were (interest-bearing) assets and hence a financial investment.

In 1947 there was a "currency reform" which discriminated against cash holdings. This, no doubt, disposed the population toward savings banks as a method of saving. Prior to the 1961 currency reform, the population, remembering its 1947 experience, may have shifted some of its cash balances to savings accounts.[42] The 1961 reform was not discriminatory, but simply made one new ruble equal ten old ones.[43]

Notes

1. Emily Clark Brown, *Soviet Trade Unions and Labor Relations,* p. 5.
2. Edmund Nash, "Recent Changes in Labor Controls in the Soviet Union," p. 854.
3. Murray Feshbach and Stephen Rapawy, "Labor Constraints in the Five-Year Plan," p. 543.
4. Brown, *Soviet Trade Unions,* p. 16.
5. Gertrude E. Schroeder, "Labor Planning in the U.S.S.R.," p. 67.
6. Alec Nove, *The Soviet Economy,* p. 27.
7. In the Soviet Union there is also the "social wage." This includes various state-provided benefits. See Schroeder, "An Appraisal of Soviet Wage and Income Statistics," pp. 295–96.
8. Schroeder, "Labor Planning," p. 69.
9. Robert M. Fearn, "Controls over Wage Funds and Inflationary Pressures in the U.S.S.R."
10. For example, they state that "in contrast to the previous pattern of a 3

to 4 percent annual average rate of growth of industrial employment, the current plan calls for only about 1.3 percent per year." And ". . . by 1967 there was a shortage of 125,000 industrial-production personnel relative to plan requirements." See Feshbach and Rapawy, "Labor Constraints," pp. 485-86.

11. Nove, *The Soviet Economy,* p. 167.

12. Feshbach and Rapawy, "Labor Constraints," pp. 490-91.

13. Feshbach, "Manpower in the U.S.S.R.: A Survey of Recent Trends and Prospects," p. 707.

14. Margaret Miller, *Rise of the Russian Consumer,* pp. 132-33.

15. Nove, *The Soviet Economy,* p. 30.

16. Ibid.

17. Marshall I. Goldman, *Soviet Marketing,* pp. 49-50.

18. Ibid., p. 182.

19. Philip Hanson, *The Consumer in the Soviet Economy,* p. 95.

20. Ibid., pp. 150-51. See also David W. Bronson and Barbara S. Severin, "Soviet Consumer Welfare: The Brezhnev Era," p. 386, on the amount of time spent shopping.

21. Bronson and Severin, "Recent Trends in Consumption and Disposable Money Income in the U.S.S.R.," p. 515.

22. Bronson and Severin, "Soviet Consumer Welfare," p. 388.

23. Hanson, *The Consumer,* pp. 38, 119.

24. Ibid., p. 62.

25. Bronson and Severin, "Soviet Consumer Welfare," pp. 384, 388.

26. Nove, *The Soviet Economy,* p. 151; Bronson and Severin, "Recent Trends," pp. 505-8; and Hanson, *The Consumer,* p. 38, describe these waiting lists or queues, or both.

27. Schroeder, "Consumer Problems and Prospects," p. 11.

28. Hanson, *The Consumer,* p. 185.

29. Ibid., p. 201.

30. Nove, *The Soviet Economy,* pp. 152, 190-91.

31. Ibid., pp. 150-53. There was a large rise in meat and milk prices in 1962 which was met by "loud protests" from consumers. See Nove, *An Economic History of the U.S.S.R.,* p. 365.

32. Nove, *The Soviet Economy,* p. 151.

33. Hanson, *The Consumer,* p. 170.

34. Besides the works cited, other sources on the Soviet official retail market include Janet G. Chapman, *Real Wages in Soviet Russia since 1928.*

35. Ibid., p. 15.

36. See, for example, Nove, *The Soviet Economy,* pp. 61-64, for a brief account of some policy changes.

37. Roy D. Laird, "The Politics of Soviet Agriculture," p. 270; Herbert J. Ellison, "Commentary," pp. 132-33.

38. Another free market is the black market. This market, although illegal,

seems to be fairly important in the Soviet Union. One of its main activities is the resale, at higher prices, of goods bought from the state and cooperative retail stores.

Besides the works cited, other sources on the Soviet collective farm market include Bronson and Severin, "Recent Trends" and "Soviet Consumer Welfare"; Goldman, *Soviet Marketing;* Jerzy F. Karcz, "Seven Years on the Farm: Retrospect and Prospects"; and Leslie Symons, *Russian Agriculture.*

39. George Garvy, *Money, Banking, and Credit in Eastern Europe,* p. 125.

40. Bronson and Severin, "Recent Trends," p. 515, note 1.

41. Miller, *Rise of the Russian Consumer,* pp. 116–20.

42. Hanson, *The Consumer,* p. 175. Hanson says that it "appears" that in 1960 there was a "once-for-all transfer from cash hoards to savings bank deposits . . ." and some stockpiling of "non-food goods."

43. Besides the works cited, other sources on the Soviet savings system include David Gallik, Cestmir Jesina, and Rapawy, *The Soviet Financial System: Structure, Operation, and Statistics;* Nash, "Recent Changes in Labor Controls"; Nove, *The Soviet Economy* and *An Economic History;* and Raymond P. Powell, "Monetary Statistics."

4

Theoretical Model

The Individual Consumer

In the Soviet economy the availability of consumer goods can be regarded as a policy parameter because the government's important role as a supplier enables it to vary the amount of consumer goods offered for sale in the state sector. Soviet policy has been to emphasize capital-goods production at the expense of consumer goods. Because of the policy of fixing the prices of many of these consumer goods at below market-clearing levels, shortages have been common. The effect of such shortages on consumer decisions about consumption and labor supply is the principal subject of this chapter. Before we address the main issue, however, rationing theory must be developed briefly.

In Tobin's 1952 survey article on the theory of rationing he presents some results derived by Tobin and Houthakker for the case of straight rationing (where a ration currency or coupon is applicable to only one commodity).[1] These are examined more carefully in the next paragraph. As Tobin states, these results strictly hold only when the "starting point" is one "common to a free market regime and to a regime of rationing."[2] That is, the only point where they are valid is a free market equilibrium. Thus Tobin and Houthakker define the rationed amount of a good to be equal to the amount which would be freely demanded otherwise, clearly a special case. Tobin also discusses the adverse effects of rationing on labor incentives.[3]

Tobin and Houthakker present many interesting and useful results. For present purposes only one is relevant. This is the prediction that "a reduction in the . . . ration—prices and income remaining unchanged—will increase the consumption of unrationed substitutes and diminish the demand for unrationed complements."[4]

Tobin and Houthakker's model has the consumer maximizing his utility function $U(x_1, \ldots, x_n)$ subject to

$$\sum_{i=1}^{n} p_i x_i = Y \quad \text{and} \quad x_k = q_k$$

for $k = m + 1, \ldots, n$, where the symbols have their usual meanings and q_k is the ration of the kth good. First-order conditions used by Tobin and Houthakker are

$$x_k = q_k \qquad k = m + 1, \ldots, n$$

and

$$\sum_{i=1}^{n} p_i x_i = Y$$

$$U_i = \lambda p_i \qquad i = 1, \ldots, m$$

where λ is the Lagrange multiplier. From these conditions the authors derive and prove their results. As will be seen, a more general formulation of the problem, involving inequalities in the quantity constraints, adds another set of conditions

$$U_i = \lambda p_i + \mu_i \qquad i = m + 1, \ldots, n$$

where the μ_i are other Lagrange multipliers. From this new system the Tobin and Houthakker results can be derived. In addition, as will be seen, the results can be extended to include disequilibrium points as well.

In a more recent paper, Pollak has introduced what he calls a "conditional demand function" in which quantities of some goods appear as arguments. Later in this chapter demand functions with quantities as arguments are developed which are in many ways similar to Pollak's conditional demand functions. For present purposes it is sufficient to note that Pollak uses these functions to derive proofs of the Tobin and Houthakker results. However, his proofs are also "valid only if the ration constraint for each rationed good is set at the free market equilibrium level of that good."[5]

The proofs in Tobin and Houthakker and in Pollak, although interesting exercises, are of limited usefulness since they apply just to a special case that is not likely to occur. The analysis presented in this chapter applies to disequilibrium points as well as to the Tobin and Houthakker special case. Thus the analysis generalizes certain predictions of rationing theory so that they apply to instances which are likely to occur under a regime of rationing. Furthermore, the analysis can be used to derive predictions about macroeconomic disequilibrium as well.

In the Soviet Union, a common phenomenon has been the case where price controls have resulted in excess demand. In such a case some consumers, perhaps all, end up facing quantity constraints on some markets in that they cannot purchase all that they would like at the going (controlled) price. This quantity-constrained situation can be expressed in a model similar to that of rationing.

Under normal circumstances the consumer exchanges his services for commodities and claims on future commodities in a manner calculated to maximize his particular utility function. For simplicity here and because of the irrelevance of other financial assets to the Soviet case, all forms of claims on future commodities will be lumped together as money balances and called savings. Similarly, it is assumed that the consumer has only one tradable good, his labor services.[6] The problem facing the consumer is to maximize his utility function $U(x_1, \ldots, x_n)$ subject to the budget constraint

$$p_L T - \sum_{i=1}^{n} p_i x_i \geq 0$$

where the x_i are the various commodities and, in particular, x_L is leisure and x_s is the increment to real savings.[7] The p_i are the various prices; T is the amount of time available to the consumer to allocate as he sees fit. The price of leisure p_L is usually taken to be the wage rate. This is correct when the individual is free to adjust his amount of work. However, when he is not free to do so, say when the work week is standardized, the wage rate may not equal the price which the individual places on his leisure.[8] The present analysis assumes that p_L is the perfect measure of the price of leisure. In addition, the consumer may face quantity constraints in that he cannot purchase all that he demands at the going price. These constraints can be expressed as

$$b_i \geq x_i \qquad i = 1, \ldots, n$$

where the b_i are the quantity constraints and $b_L \leq T$.

In other words, the problem is to maximize

$$U(x_1, \ldots, x_n) + \lambda \left(p_L T - \sum_{i=1}^{n} p_i x_i \right) + \sum_{i=1}^{n} \mu_i (b_i - x_i)$$

The Kuhn-Tucker conditions are the following:

$$
\left.
\begin{aligned}
U_i - \lambda p_i - \mu_i &\leq 0 & i = 1, \ldots, n \\
x_i (U_i - \lambda p_i - \mu_i) &= 0 & i = 1, \ldots, n \\
x_i &\geq 0 & i = 1, \ldots, n
\end{aligned}
\right\} i \neq s
$$

$$U_s - \lambda p_s - \mu_s = 0$$

$$x_s (U_s - \lambda p_s - \mu_s) = 0$$

x_s unrestricted,

$$p_L T - \sum_{i=1}^{n} p_i x_i \geqslant 0$$

$$\lambda \left(p_L T - \sum_{i=1}^{n} p_i x_i \right) = 0$$

$$\lambda \geqslant 0$$

$$b_i - x_i \geqslant 0 \qquad i = 1, \ldots, n$$

$$\mu_i (b_i - x_i) = 0 \qquad i = 1, \ldots, n$$

$$\mu_i \geqslant 0 \qquad i = 1, \ldots, n$$

Following convention, assume that the individual consumes some of each good (other than saving since dissaving must be allowed) that is, $x_i > 0, i \neq s$. This means that

$$U_i - \lambda p_i - \mu_i = 0 \qquad i = 1, \ldots, n$$

If no constraints are active in the sense that

$$b_i > x_i \qquad i = 1, \ldots, n$$

then this implies that

$$\mu_i = 0 \qquad i = 1, \ldots, n$$

If it is assumed that no purchasing power is thrown away, then

$$p_L T - \sum_{i=1}^{n} p_i x_i = 0$$

Thus the conventional first-order conditions can be generated:

$$U_i - \lambda p_i = 0 \qquad i = 1, \ldots, n$$

$$p_L T - \sum_{i=1}^{n} p_i x_i = 0$$

Total differentiation yields

$$[Z]\begin{bmatrix} dx_j \\ \hline d\lambda \end{bmatrix} = \begin{bmatrix} \lambda dp_j \\ \hline -p_L\, dT - T\, dp_L + \sum_{i=1}^{n} x_i\, dp_i \end{bmatrix} \quad j = 1, \ldots, n \qquad (4.1)$$

where $[Z]$ is the usual bordered Hessian matrix,

$$\begin{bmatrix} dx_j \\ \hline d\lambda \end{bmatrix} \quad \text{is} \quad [dx_1, \ldots, dx_n, d\lambda]'$$

and so on. In analyzing the quantity-constrained case, at least one of the quantity constraints is allowed to be active. The rest of the assumptions are retained.

Suppose that consumption of just one good, say x_n, is constrained in that there is a shortage of x_n. This is expressed as $x_n = b_n$ where b_n is less than or equal to the amount of x_n that is demanded at the going price under normal circumstances. Of course, when it is equal, there is no shortage. However, this case is included so that the results will include a transition from a normal economy to one with a shortage of x_n.

Thus, for the representative consumer,

$$b_i - x_i > 0 \qquad i = 1, \ldots, n-1$$
$$b_n - x_n = 0$$

which implies

$$\mu_i = 0 \qquad i = 1, \ldots, n-1$$
$$\mu_n \geqslant 0$$

(In Tobin and Houthakker's special case $\mu_n = 0$, but $b_n - x_n = 0$.) Therefore, for this constrained case the first-order conditions are[9]

$$U_i - \lambda^* p_i = 0 \qquad i = 1, \ldots, n-1$$
$$U_n - \lambda^* p_n - \mu_n = 0$$
$$p_L T - \sum_{i=1}^{n} p_i x_i = 0$$
$$b_n - x_n = 0$$

where the asterisk on λ^* indicates that the point involved is quantity-constrained. Total differentiation yields

$$[D] \begin{bmatrix} dx_j \\ \hline d\lambda^* \\ d\mu_n \end{bmatrix} = \begin{bmatrix} \lambda^* dp_j \\ \hline -p_L dT - T dp_L + \sum_{i=1}^{n} x_i dp_i \\ -db_n \end{bmatrix} \quad j = 1, \ldots, n \qquad (4.2)$$

where $[D]$ is $[Z]$ with the additional border $(0, \ldots, 0, -1, 0, 0)$.
Consider

$$\frac{\delta x_1}{\delta b_n} = \frac{(-1)D_{n+2,1}}{D}$$

where D is the determinant of $[D]$ and D_{ij} is the cofactor of the ith row and jth column of that determinant. To evaluate $\delta x_1/\delta b_n$, first define Z to be the determinant of $[Z]$ and Z_{ij} as the minor of the ith row and jth column of Z. Since

$$D_{n+2,1} = (-1)^{n+1} Z_{n1} \quad \text{and} \quad D = (-1)Z_{nn}$$

$$\frac{\delta x_1}{\delta b_n} = \frac{(-1)^{n+1} Z_{n1}}{Z_{nn}}$$

When there are no quantity constraints, utility maximization yields first-order conditions that, when totally differentiated, yield equation (4.1). In such a situation, the compensated substitution effect of a change in p_n is

$$\left(\frac{\delta x_1}{\delta p_n} \right)_{U \text{ const}} = \frac{\lambda (-1)^{n+1} Z_{n1}}{Z} \qquad (4.3)$$

The second-order conditions include

$$(-1)^{n-1} Z_{nn} > 0 \quad (-1)^n Z > 0 \qquad (4.4)$$

If the utility function is quasi-concave (which is assumed to be the case), these conditions are satisfied. In fact, if the function is quasi-concave, these second-order conditions are satisfied for a range of values of the x_i. Thus in this range a determinant of any given dimension will have the same sign regardless of the quantities used to evaluate it, as long as the prices remain the same.

From the first-order conditions it can be shown that the Lagrange multipliers

λ and λ^* are positive since goods are economic goods (that is, $U_i > 0$ and $p_i > 0$, $i = 1, \ldots, n$). With this knowledge plus equation (4.4), the relationship between $\delta x_1/\delta b_n$ and $(\delta x_1/\delta p_n)_{U \text{ const}}$ can be determined. (The asterisk indicates that the expression is evaluated at the constrained point.)

$$\frac{\delta x_1/\delta b_n}{(\delta x_1/\delta p_n)_{U \text{ const}}} = \frac{1}{\lambda} \cdot \frac{Z^*_{n1}}{Z^*_{nn}} \cdot \frac{Z}{Z_{n1}}$$

From (4.4) and the discussion following (4.4), if the two points being considered are within the range where $U(\cdot)$ is quasi-concave [or if $U(\cdot)$ is globally quasi-concave], then Z^*_{nn} and Z are of opposite sign. Therefore (since $\lambda > 0$)

$$\text{sign} \left[\frac{\delta x_1/\delta b_n}{(\delta x_1/\delta p_n)_{U \text{ const}}} \right] = \text{sign} \, (-1) \, Z^*_{n1}/Z_{n1}$$

For the case of Tobin-Houthakker rationing, that is, where the x_i as well as the p_i are the same in the constrained and unconstrained cases, the numerator and denominator on the right-hand side of the equation are equal. Thus

$$\left[\frac{\delta x_1/\delta b_n}{(\delta x_1/\delta p_n)_{U \text{ const}}} \right] < 0$$

That is, $\delta x_1/\delta b_n$ and $(\delta x_1/\delta p_n)_{U \text{ const}}$ are of opposite sign. Therefore, for Hicks-Allen substitutes, $\delta x_1/\delta b_n < 0$; for complements, $\delta x_1/\delta b_n > 0$. A proof of these predictions for this special case is given by Tobin and Houthakker.[10] However, it will be shown here that the predictions hold under much more general conditions.

To prove that $(\delta x_1/\delta b_n)/(\delta x_1/\delta p_n)_{U \text{ const}}$ is negative in the general case, it must be shown that Z^*_{n1} and Z_{n1} have the same sign. A reasonable definition of a disequilibrium substitution effect would be

$$\left(\frac{\delta x^*_1}{\delta p_n} \right)_{U \text{ const}} = \frac{\lambda^{**}(-1)^{n+1} Z^*_{n1}}{Z^*}$$

where the expression is evaluated at the disequilibrium point, but without holding the quantity constraint active (this is indicated by the double asterisk on λ^{**}). By comparing this effect to an equilibrium substitution effect, for example, (4.3), it can be seen that, since the denominators have the same sign in both cases [from the conditions of (4.4)] if the points are within the range where $U(\cdot)$ is quasi-concave, then Z^*_{n1} and Z_{n1} will have the same sign ($\lambda^{**} > 0$) if goods 1 and n have the same substitutability/complementarity relationship to each other in disequilibrium as they do in equilibrium. Goods that are substitutes in equilibrium are defined as substitutes in disequilibrium for the purposes of this book if these determinants are of the same sign, and likewise for complements. Thus, as long as relationships remain the same,

$$\left[\frac{\delta x_1/\delta b_n}{(\delta x_1/\delta p_n)_{U \text{ const}}} \right] < 0$$

and the predictions derived above that $\delta x_1/\delta b_n < 0$ for substitutes and $\delta x_1/\delta b_n > 0$ for complements hold generally.[11] Thus, for substitutes, if available x_n decreases (increases), demand for x_1 increases (decreases), and so on.[12]

Implicit in the first-order conditions of the constrained-consumption utility maximization problem (assuming that the implicit functions exist) is a set of equations[13] relating the dependent variables x_i to all the parameters involved:

$$x_i = f_i(b_n, p_1, \ldots, p_n, T) = g_i(b_n, p_1, \ldots, p_n) \quad i = 1, \ldots, n-1 \quad (4.5)$$

These represent the individual's demand functions for x_i. The analysis has already determined the sign of the partial derivative with respect to b_n. The signs of the partial derivatives with respect to prices must now be determined.[14]

From (4.2) can be derived (for $i = 1, \ldots, n-1$)

$$\frac{\delta x_i}{\delta p_i} = \frac{\lambda^* D_{ii}}{D} + \frac{x_i D_{n+1,i}}{D} \quad i \neq L$$

$$\frac{\delta x_i}{\delta p_L} = \frac{\lambda^* D_{Li}}{D} + \frac{(x_L - T) D_{n+1,i}}{D}$$

$$\frac{\delta x_i}{\delta p_m} = \frac{\lambda^* D_{mi}}{D} + \frac{x_m D_{n+1,i}}{D}$$

$$\frac{\delta x_i}{\delta p_n} = \frac{\lambda^* D_{ni}}{D} + \frac{x_n D_{n+1,i}}{D}$$

The term $-D_{n+1,i}/D$ can be interpreted as an income effect,[15] and assuming that all goods are normal, it is defined to be positive.

The second-order conditions for a maximum require that (because $\lambda^* > 0$ as shown previously)

$$\lambda^* D_{ii}/D < 0 \quad i = 1, \ldots, n-1$$

The signs of D_{Li} ($i \neq L$) and D_{mi} ($i \neq m$) are indeterminate. However, there does not seem to be any reason why the introduction of a quantity constraint should affect substitution relationships between unconstrained goods. Since, by elimination, $\lambda^* D_{Li}/D$ and $\lambda^* D_{mi}/D$ can be interpreted as substitution effects, their signs can be determined. They are positive if the goods involved are substitutes, negative if they are complements. Inspection of (4.2) leads to the conclusion that $D_{ni} = 0$ because of the expansion of the determinants by a column of zeros. This is because the constraint $x_n = b_n$ allows no adjustment in real consumption of the nth good; thus the only effect is an income effect on the consumption of other goods.

Based on the above information, the signs of the partial derivatives are (for $i = 1, \ldots, n - 1$)

$$\delta x_i/\delta p_i < 0 \quad i \neq L, s$$

$$\delta x_L/\delta p_L \lessgtr 0$$

$$\delta x_s/\delta p_s \lessgtr 0$$

$$\left.\begin{array}{l} \delta x_i/\delta p_L > 0 \\ \delta x_i/\delta p_m \lessgtr 0 \end{array}\right\} \text{for Hicks-Allen substitutes} \qquad (4.6)$$

$$\left.\begin{array}{l} \delta x_i/\delta p_L \lessgtr 0 \\ \delta x_i/\delta p_m < 0 \quad m \neq s \\ \delta x_i/\delta p_s \lessgtr 0 \\ \delta x_i/\delta p_n < 0 \end{array}\right\} \text{for Hicks-Allen complements}$$

Thus the present analysis yields predictions about quantity-constrained situations in general, not just the Tobin-Houthakker special case. Furthermore, the analysis can be used to study macroeconomic disequilibrium. The prediction that $\delta x_1/\delta b_n < 0$ for substitutes is especially useful in the study of macroeconomic disequilibrium.

This analysis can be used in the Keynesian case of general disequilibrium with excess supply of labor, that is, unemployment. Following Clower,[16] the consumer can be viewed as facing a constraint on his labor supply. In terms of the Kuhn-Tucker conditions, the last three become

$$\left.\begin{array}{ll} b_i - x_i \geqslant 0 & i = 1, \ldots, n \\ \mu_i(b_i - x_i) = 0 & i = 1, \ldots, n \\ \mu_i \geqslant 0 & i = 1, \ldots, n \end{array}\right\} i \neq L$$

$$b_L - x_L \leqslant 0$$

$$\mu_L(b_L - x_L) = 0$$

$$\mu_L \leqslant 0$$

When there is unemployment, then $b_L - x_L = 0$ and the analysis proceeds as in the case of a shortage of good n. The results hold, that is, $\delta x_1/\delta b_L < 0$ for substitutes, and so on. In this case the functions are

$$x_i = h_i(b_L, p_1, \ldots, p_n) \qquad i \neq L$$

The present analysis predicts that if good i and leisure are Hicks-Allen substitutes, then

$$\frac{\delta x_i}{\delta b_L} < 0$$

In most cases this will probably be so since most consumption goods are probably substitutes for pure leisure.

The analysis shows the choice-theoretic basis of the Keynesian consumption function with its assertion that consumption is a positive function of income (if there is involuntary unemployment).[17] Keynes's assertion depends on the substitutability of consumption goods and leisure. Actually, his assertion just requires what might be called "net" substitutability since he does not talk about individual consumption goods but rather one composite consumption good. The present analysis, therefore, shows the actual basis of the Keynesian consumption function—the assumption of substitutability of consumption goods and leisure and the existence of a quantity constraint in the labor market.

Equations (4.5) are not exactly those proposed by Barro and Grossman. Recall from chapter 2 that their functions include the real wage and real money balances. The above equations can be easily expressed in relative-price form—thus incorporating, *inter alia,* a real wage—by interpreting the p_i as being divided by the general price level. Thus, all the above results hold, but the ones involving changes in p_s can be ignored since when the p_i are interpreted as "real" prices, p_s is always 1. The stock of savings was excluded from the analysis because Tobin and Houthakker did not include it in theirs. However, real savings can be put into the equations very easily.

One way of inserting real savings into the demand functions is to postulate a utility function containing the total stock of real savings at the end of the period rather than just the period's flow of saving. This is the method used by Barro and Grossman (see chapter 2). Thus, if X_s denotes the real value of savings and $X_{s_{-1}}$ is the real value of savings carried over from the previous period, and since $x_s = X_s - X_{s_{-1}}$, then X_s replaces x_s in the household's utility function, and the budget constraint becomes

$$p_L T + p_s X_{s_{-1}} - \sum_{\substack{i=1, \\ i \neq s}}^{n} p_i x_i - p_s X_s \geq 0 \qquad (4.7)$$

In such a case equation set (4.2) is changed in just two respects: X_s replaces x_s, and the second-to-last line on the right-hand side becomes

$$-p_L\, dT - T\, dp_L - (X_{s_{-1}}\, dp_s + p_s\, dX_{s_{-1}}) + \sum_{\substack{i=1,\\ i \neq s}}^{n} x_i\, dp_i + X_s\, dp_s$$

As can be seen, the qualitative properties of the response predictions are unaffected by the presence of $X_{s_{-1}}$. However, the signs of

$$\frac{\delta x_i}{\delta X_{s_{-1}}} \quad \text{and} \quad \frac{\delta X_s}{\delta X_{s_{-1}}} \quad i = 1, \ldots, n-1; i \neq s$$

must be determined. Since

$$\frac{\delta x_i}{\delta X_{s_{-1}}} = \frac{-p_s D_{n+1,i}}{D} \quad i = 1, \ldots, n-1; i \neq s$$

and similarly for $\delta X_s / \delta X_{s_{-1}}$, a change in $X_{s_{-1}}$ is analogous to an income effect (see note 15). Thus,

$$\frac{\delta x_i}{\delta X_{s_{-1}}} > 0 \quad i = 1, \ldots, n-1; i \neq s$$

$$\frac{\delta X_s}{\delta X_{s_{-1}}} > 0$$

This discussion has demonstrated how equations (4.5) are transformed into

$$\begin{aligned} x_i &= g_i(b_n, p_j, X_{s_{-1}}) \quad i = 1, \ldots, n-1; i \neq s \\ X_s &= g_s(b_n, p_j, X_{s_{-1}}) \quad j = 1, \ldots, n; j \neq s \end{aligned} \tag{4.8}$$

Equations (4.8) are like those of Barro and Grossman except that Barro and Grossman have a *saving* function rather than a *savings* function. The linear form of $g_s(\cdot)$ can be transformed easily into a saving function by subtracting $X_{s_{-1}}$ from both sides. Predictions remain the same except that the sign of $\delta x_s / \delta X_{s_{-1}}$ is indeterminate. However, if one does not replace x_s with X_s in the utility function, but simply writes the constraint as in (4.7), then the sign of $\delta x_s / \delta X_{s_{-1}}$ becomes determinate (positive).

The model can be simplified by assuming that there are four goods: leisure $T - L^s$, where L^s is labor supplied; a constrained consumption good B^0; an unconstrained consumption good A^d; and real saving s^d. The prices of these goods are, respectively, the nominal wage rate W, the money prices of B^0 and A^d (P^B and P^A), and the general price level P. The nominal value of savings carried over from last period is H_{-1}. This is similar to Barro and Grossman's model except for the addition of A^d. There are now only three equations which relate the unknowns L^s (or $T - L^s$), A^d, and s^d to the variables B^0 (which is, of course, the equivalent of b_n in the above analysis), H_{-1}/P, and the relative prices W/P, P^B/P, and P^A/P. These represent the individual's supply of labor, demand for the unconstrained consumption good, and demand for saving functions, respectively. These are written for the jth individual as

$$^jL^s = {}^jL^s({}^jB^0, {}^jH_{-1}/P, W/P, P^B/P, P^A/P) \qquad (4.9)$$

$$^jA^d = {}^jA^d({}^jB^0, {}^jH_{-1}/P, W/P, P^B/P, P^A/P) \qquad (4.10)$$

$$^js^d = {}^js^d({}^jB^0, {}^jH_{-1}/P, W/P, P^B/P, P^A/P) \qquad (4.11)$$

Recall from the above that when the functions were of the form

$$x_i = g_i(b_n, p_j, X_{s_{-1}}) \qquad i = 1, \ldots, n-1; j = 1, \ldots, n; j \neq s$$

it was found that for substitutes $\delta x_i/\delta b_n < 0$. Therefore if leisure, consumption goods, and saving are all (Hicks-Allen) substitutes for one another, then by analogy with these general results the partial derivatives of the simplified functions with respect to $^jB^0$ are

$$\frac{\delta(T - {}^jL^s)}{\delta^jB^0} = -\frac{\delta^jL^s}{\delta^jB^0} < 0$$

or

$$\frac{\delta^jL^s}{\delta^jB^0} > 0$$

and

$$\frac{\delta^jA^d}{\delta^jB^0} < 0 \qquad \frac{\delta^js^d}{\delta^jB^0} < 0$$

That is, in times of shortages of consumer goods, or excess commodity demand, when B^0 decreases (increases), the analysis predicts that labor supply also decreases (increases), and the demands for unconstrained consumption goods and for future claims increase (decrease). These results include those of Barro and Grossman for the case of excess demand.[18] The present analysis provides the choice-theoretic basis of these results as well. In addition, it shows the importance of the assumption in Barro and Grossman's model that leisure, consumption goods, and saving are substitutes. The substitutability between leisure and consumption would hold in most normal situations. However, the assumption that consumption and "money" are substitutes would seem to preclude a strictly transactions use of money. Therefore what they call money should be regarded as savings and is so designated throughout this analysis.

The signs of the various price effects in the simplified functions can be easily determined from (4.6). Since

$$\frac{\delta x_L}{\delta p_L} \leqq 0$$

then $\delta L^s / \delta (W/P)$ will also be indeterminate. Since

$$\frac{\delta x_i}{\delta p_i} < 0 \qquad i \neq L, s$$

other own-price effects will be negative. Because all goods in the system are substitutes, other-price effects will be

$$\frac{\delta x_i}{\delta p_L} > 0$$

$$\frac{\delta x_i}{\delta p_m} \leqq 0 \qquad i = 1, \dots, n - 1$$

$$\frac{\delta x_i}{\delta p_n} < 0$$

Therefore all other-price effects with respect to W/P and P^B/P are positive and negative, respectively, and all others are indeterminate. Note that $x_L = T - L^s$; hence the conclusions about signs of partial derivatives of L^s are the opposite of those about x_L (as shown explicitly in regard to $\delta x_L / \delta b_n$).

The signs of the partial derivatives with respect to $^j H_{-1}/P$ are analogous to those involving $X_{s_{-1}}$ in the above analysis. Thus, they are negative for $^j L^s$, positive for A^d, and either positive or indeterminate for s^d depending on the assumption made about the household's utility function.

The predictions as to the signs of the responses to changes in the right-hand variables are summarized in table 4-1.

Table 4–1
Predicted Signs

	$^jL^s$	$^jA^d$	$^js^d$
$^jB^0$	+	–	–
$^jH_{-1}/P$	–	+	?
w/P	?	+	+
p^B/P	+	–	–
p^A/P	?	–	?

Equations (4.9) to (4.11) represent individual behavior. In order to derive hypotheses about aggregate behavior, one must sum over all individuals. This is done in the next section. Before moving on, note the existence of current transactions $^jB^0$ in the functions. Thus, these functions could be called Keynesian in the sense discussed by Clower (see chapter 2).

Aggregation

As Green states in his survey of the aggregation problem,

> In the broadest sense, aggregation is a process whereby a part of the information available for the solution of a problem is sacrificed for the purpose of making the problem more easily manageable. . . . Aggregation will be judged satisfactory by the economist to the extent that he believes that the cost of handling information in greater detail outweighs the greater reliability of the results he might obtain by using more detailed information; the judgement must depend, of course, on the purpose of the investigation.[19]

In the present case the cost of handling the detailed information is truly prohibitive. There is no way of observing each individual household. Therefore it is necessary to use totals, averages, index numbers, and the like in the empirical work, recognizing that this may introduce an aggregation bias. Furthermore, the purpose of this book is to derive macroeconomic relations among such aggregate data. Thus on both of Green's criteria, equations (4.9) to (4.11) should be aggregated over all individual households.

In order to aggregate the relations, first define

$$L^s = \sum_{j=1}^{N} {}^jL^s \qquad A^d = \sum_{j=1}^{N} {}^jA^d \qquad s^d = \sum_{j=1}^{N} {}^js^d$$

$$B^0 = \sum_{j=1}^{N} {}^{j}B^0 \quad \text{and} \quad H_{-1} = \sum_{j=1}^{N} {}^{j}H_{-1}$$

where N is the number of households. The familiar macroeconomic assumption of no distribution effects leads to the following aggregate functions:

$$L^s = L^s(B^0, H_{-1}/P,\ W/P,\ P^B/P,\ P^A/P) \tag{4.12}$$

$$A^d = A^d(B^0, H_{-1}/P,\ W/P,\ P^B/P,\ P^A/P) \tag{4.13}$$

$$s^d = s^d(B^0, H_{-1}/P,\ W/P,\ P^B/P,\ P^A/P) \tag{4.14}$$

The assumption of no distribution effects means that the predicted signs of the partial derivatives remain the same as in table 4-1.

The second aggregation problem arises in giving empirical meaning to the five variables L^s, A^d, s^d, H_{-1}, and B^0. In order to do this, one must aggregate the many goods in a modern economy into composite goods. L^s is a summation of labor time, and s^d and H_{-1} are summations of money. In the application of the model to the Soviet Union (see "Application of the Model to the Soviet Economy" for details) goods sold on a free market are identified as A^d and those sold by the state at fixed prices as B^0. The empirical work considers A^d to be comprised of goods sold on the collective farm market. This selection of composite goods is made of necessity. Use of composite goods is common in economics even though the formal conditions under which such goods can be used are very stringent.

The Simultaneous System

In the preceding analysis, the macroeconomic functions (4.12) to (4.14) have been carefully derived. These functions are to be estimated in order to test the model's predictions. However, there are endogenous variables on the right-hand side, specifically W, P^A, and P. These are the outcomes of market or marketlike processes, whereas B^0 and P^B are state policy parameters, and H_{-1} is predetermined. In the individual household's functions, all six variables on the right-hand side are exogenous since the individual household is a price taker. In the aggregate case W, P^A, and P cannot be taken as given because they are simultaneously determined with, among other things, L^s, A^d, and s^d. In order to estimate (4.12) to (4.14) properly, the rest of the simultaneous system must be specified. Because the present purpose is not to estimate the remaining functions in the system, but rather to use them to obtain consistent estimates of (4.12) to (4.14), it is not necessary to devote a great deal of space to deriving them.

The decision to produce and market collective farm market goods will depend on relative prices, the real value of savings, and the availability of other goods to buy with the proceeds of sales on this market. In addition, government policy (G) can and does affect supply on the collective farm market, and, of course, weather (R) does also. Thus

$$A^s = A^s(B^0, H_{-1}/P, W/P, P^B/P, P^A/P, G, R) \tag{4.15}$$

$$A^d = A^s \tag{4.16}$$

The enterprise sector in the Soviet economy has the production function (the symbols have their usual meanings) $Q = g(K, L)$. Capital is mostly allocated on a physical basis to each enterprise by the central authorities. Thus K can be treated as an exogenous variable. The output level Q is determined mostly (if not entirely) by state policy parameters, namely the output plan and the managerial incentive scheme. Thus it, too, can be treated as exogenous. Therefore $L = h(Q^0, K^0)$, where L is labor needed to produce Q^0. It is asserted here that the demand for labor is related to this labor needed and the wage rate (see chapter 3). Hence the demand for labor function is

$$L^d = L^d(W/P, Q^0, K^0) \tag{4.17}$$

where Q^0 is total output and so on. Also,

$$L^s = L^d \tag{4.18}$$

In this model the general price level is a weighted average of the prices of the two types of consumption goods in the model;

$$P = \lambda_1 P^A + \lambda_2 P^B \tag{4.19}$$

Thus, there are eight unknowns $(L^s, A^d, s^d, A^s, L^d, P, W, P^A)$, seven exogenous variables $(B^0, P^B, H_{-1}, G, R, K^0, Q^0)$—recall that B^0 and P^B are policy variables—and eight equations.

Application of the Model to the Soviet Economy

The purpose of this section is to apply the equations developed in earlier sections to the Soviet economy. In the Soviet Union, the household faces many nonmarket-clearing prices which typically are too low. These therefore generate shortages. This was discussed in chapter 3. Furthermore, the households have freedom of action in certain directions. Specifically, they are free to choose what goods to buy from among those supplied by the state sector on the official retail market; they are free to buy and sell on the collective farm market; they can save; and they have some freedom in the labor market in terms of place of work, turnover, and so on. In such a situation, the disequilibrium analysis developed here to investigate the implications of quantity constraints (in this case, shortages) on economic behavior is relevant.

A brief description of the variables is given here; a more detailed discussion is presented in chapter 6. B^0 is defined to be all those goods and services provided by the state sector (hence it is a government policy parameter). These are sold at prices P^B, which are inflexible and only casually related to the forces of supply and demand.

Time worked as an employee is L^s (in one measure this includes private employment), and W is the average wage. The real increment in personal savings accounts is defined to be s^d; H_{-1} is the nominal stock of these accounts prevailing at the beginning of the period.

There are at least three groups of goods in the Soviet Union that should be included in A^d: agricultural goods sold on the collective farm market, personal services (supplied privately), and goods supplied through the black market. All these have market-determined prices. Conceptually all three can be included in A^d with little problem. However, only sales on the collective farm market are reported, so in empirical work the last two must be excluded. Therefore, A^d is measured by sales on the collective farm market, and P^A is the price of goods sold on this market.[20] P is a price index constructed using P^B and P^A.

It is important that the household's options, that is, its economic environment, be correctly specified. Several questions can be raised about the specification implicit in this model. In the Soviet Union, as in probably every other country, the household has the option of producing for its own consumption (and for sale). However, it is likely that this is more important in the Soviet economy than in other developed economies. This type of behavior is included indirectly in the model. The leisure variable in the main specification of L^s is actually time not worked as an official employee. Thus time spent on private production is included in leisure,[21] except when total civilian employment is used as L^s (see chapter 6). Decisions with regard to private production are reflected primarily in the L^s, A^d, and A^s functions. Because of the specification of L^s, the prediction as to direction of response is unaffected by such things as decreases in employment being partially offset by increases in work on private production. (In the main case, the prediction is unaffected even if there are completely offsetting effects.) This book is interested only in market behavior, not in measuring real consumption or welfare, and for this purpose the phenomenon of private production is covered sufficiently.

A potential problem arises if rates of return on time differ, as when the wage rate differs from what the household can earn for its time spent on private production. Clearly, this is not the only way in which rates of return on time can differ. There can also be an unofficial wage (perhaps illegal) which is not equal to the official wage. Furthermore, standardized work weeks can generally be expected to make the wage rate differ from the price which the household places on its leisure. In the Soviet Union, labor coercion can make this a more serious problem than it is in the West. In the case of the individual consumer, this problem is easily solved by using a different price of leisure for each consumer and by not specifying it to be a wage rate. (Thus the models would have ${}^j p_L$ and ${}^j W$, $j = 1, \ldots, N$.) However, in the aggregate case one must abstract from this problem and assume that there are no distribution effects, and thus assume that the average price of leisure adequately measures the effects of all the individual prices of leisure. In the empirical work of this book, it must be assumed further that the average wage rate is an adequate measure of the average price of leisure.

Another problem is the treatment of black markets for the same goods sold legally on other markets. In the disaggregated model one simply postulates another good x_{i+n} to be the amount of x_i sold on the black market. Thus one could conceivably have $2n$ goods in the model. Since these black-market goods have different nonprice characteristics, for example, ease of purchase and legal risks, different prices, and are sold on different markets, they can be treated as separate goods. In the aggregate model these black-market goods are omitted because of the lack of data on them. The existence of the two markets would lead to a tendency toward "encroachment," as Boulding has pointed out.[22] That is, supplies would be transferred from the state market to the free market, and eventually the whole retail market would become a free one. This has not occurred in the Soviet Union mainly because of the rules and laws against such "speculation."

A possible problem arises in that the rural sector was remonetized to a large extent during the present period of study. How does this affect the supply and demand functions? To the extent that remonetization resulted in an increase in the wages paid to agricultural workers, it is reflected by changes in wages. Since the possibility of reselling was open to the peasant, there is no reason (aside from differences in transaction costs) why consumption patterns would be affected one way or the other by the switch from in-kind payments to money payments (as long as they were of equal value). Relative prices and availabilities of goods may change, but these effects are already accounted for in the functions. Rural monetization per se does not affect the model's demand functions.

In the first section of this chapter the role of expectations in an intertemporal utility maximization process was mentioned. In the model this mostly reduces to the question of the effects of expectations on the saving-versus-leisure decision. A household will be more inclined to save its excess purchasing power rather than cut its labor supply if it expects there to be relatively more consumer goods available in the future than there are now. The economy's present output mix affects these expectations. If the economy persistently produces unwanted consumer goods, this inclines the household toward taking leisure rather than saving because it seems likely to the household that there will not be much to buy in the future also.

Similarly, the type of producer goods being made, if observable, will also affect expectations. For example, if machines for making specialized defense goods are produced rather than machines for making consumer goods, this will also incline the household toward taking increased leisure rather than increased saving as its response to shortages. So the exact response of the household to present shortages depends on expectations, and thus the determinants of those expectations, as well as the arguments which have been included in the functions.[23]

Related to this discussion is the question of whether saving is merely the means of accumulating money for large purchases and not a response to shortages at all. This is an especially relevant question for the case of the Soviet Union, which has relatively few credit arrangements for consumers. In this case an increase in the availability of expensive consumer goods will directly increase saving and perhaps create expectations of more availability in the future as well and thereby induce still more saving. In this case the prediction is the opposite of what the present model predicts. No doubt, expectations functions could be devised for this and the general leisure-saving choice discussed in the preceding paragraph. However, this book does not pursue the subject further, although it seems clear that expectations will influence the relative sizes of the elasticities of response.[24]

In conclusion, it can be said that the Soviet household is free to maximize its utility subject to certain constraints. These constraints are mainly quantity constraints (shortages) which result from the fact that prices for a set of consumer goods are too low relative to demand for them. This book investigates the implications of these incorrect prices on aggregate household behavior; for this purpose, a version of the basic Barro-Grossman disequilibrium model is used.

Notes

1. James Tobin, "A Survey of the Theory of Rationing"; Tobin and H.S. Houthakker, "The Effects of Rationing on Demand Elasticities."

2. Tobin, "Survey," p. 529.

3. Ibid., p. 538.

4. Tobin and Houthakker, "Effects of Rationing," p. 142.

5. Robert A. Pollak, "Conditional Demand Functions and Consumption Theory," p. 72.

6. Later in this chapter cases are discussed in which the household has

other options open to it, such as production for market or own consumption and trading on a secondary, perhaps illegal, market.

7. Inclusion of saving, that is, the increment to real savings, in the utility function is actually just a simplification of the real issue involved—the intertemporal maximization of utility. Saving is used as a generalized future consumption commodity. It is, in fact, a claim on future commodities. In principle, the model should dispense with this simplification and include in the utility function the (expected) dated commodities x_i^t exclusive of saving, and should include (expected) future prices in the budget constraint. However, this is not done. Instead, the analysis proceeds with the simplified utility maximization problem. Further implications of this are taken up later.

8. See Roger Sherman and Thomas D. Willett, "The Standardized Work Week and the Allocation of Time," p. 66. This problem, of course, is relevant to the Soviet Union. In fact, it may be a more serious problem there than elsewhere, where standardization and inflexibility are even more prevalent than in the West. Another complicating factor is the phenomenon of moonlighting. Any work done at unofficial wages means that the official wage rate will not represent the price of leisure (in general). For theoretical work it is assumed that p_L is the correct measure and therefore not necessarily the official (or even unofficial) wage rate. This problem is considered again later in this chapter.

9. The second-order conditions for utility maximization hold for this case.

10. Tobin and Houthakker, "Effects of Rationing."

11. For the case of many constrained goods one can proceed in one of two ways: all the constrained goods can be treated as a composite good and the above results apply. On the other hand, it can be shown that if the absence or presence of the other constrained goods does not affect the sign of $(\delta x_1/\delta p_n)_{U \text{ const}}$, then results similar to the above can be obtained. The proof is in appendix 4A.

12. The above discussion should make clearer what is meant by the use of comparative statics in a disequilibrium context. Constained equilibria are being compared. The individual is, as assumed, in his best position possible given the circumstances, which include one or more nonclearing markets. Then one conducts an experiment by changing only one parameter and observes the direction of change in the dependent variable of interest.

In the Soviet Union most of the constraints facing the consumer are policy variables. These are exogenous to the system, and there will be no economic forces tending to make them adjust to market conditions. The Soviet consumer has expectations as to possible changes in these constraints. Given these expectations, he plans his affairs accordingly in order to maximize his utility. The outcome of this process is an equilibrium of sorts in that given the prevailing conditions, the consumer cannot make himself better off and there is little or no tendency to change without an exogenous shock. Compare to Herschel I. Grossman, "Money, Interest, and Prices in Market Disequilibrium," p. 958. See also note 2 in Robert Clower, "The Keynesian Counterrevolution," p. 123.

13. Actually $i = 1, \ldots, n$, but it is specified that $x_n = b_n$ for the purpose of this analysis.

14. See Pollak, "Conditional Demand Functions," for an extensive treatment of demand functions similar to these.

15. This can be easily demonstrated. Suppose the consumer's budget is supplemented by an additional income receipt Y. Thus the budget constraint becomes

$$Y + p_L T - \sum_{i=1}^{n} p_i x_i$$

The right-hand side of (4.2) becomes

$$\begin{bmatrix} \lambda^* dp_j \\ \hline -dY - p_L\, dT - T\, dp_L + \sum_{i=1}^{n} x_i\, dp_i \\ -db_n \end{bmatrix} \quad j = 1, \ldots, n$$

Thus

$$\frac{\delta x_i}{\delta Y} = -\frac{D_{n+1,i}}{D} \quad i = 1, \ldots, n-1$$

which is what is stated in the text.

16. Clower, "The Keynesian Counterrevolution."

17. It is customary to use labor income as the quantity variable in the consumption function. However, Keynes used income for "convenience" only. The relation in which he was truly interested was that between consumption and employment. (See John Maynard Keynes, *The General Theory of Employment, Interest, and Money*, p. 90.) Thus the functions used here are, presumably, what he "really" had in mind. In any case, they are derivable from a utility maximization model with quantity constraints.

18. Robert J. Barro and Grossman, "A General Disequilibrium Model of Income and Employment," p. 91.

19. H.A. John Green, *Aggregation in Economic Analysis: An Introductory Survey*, p. 3.

20. Thus, if elasticities for food differ from those of services and black-market goods, the empirical system misses vital information. As is well known, the composition of a society's demand for agricultural goods and for services

generally changes as its economy develops. However, in the short period studied here, one can expect there to be a minimum of such structural change in demand.

21. Time spent in queues, that is, transactions time, is also included.

22. Kenneth Boulding, "A Note on the Theory of the Black Market."

23. The Soviet authorities seem to be well aware of this, as evidenced by their use of well-publicized and spectacular projects, such as apartment houses, to give the households hope of more to consume in the future.

24. The model leaves out the rate of interest paid on savings deposits because it did not vary during the period of study; hence one can simplify the model at no cost.

Appendix 4A

There are $n - k + 1$ constrained goods and $k - 1$ unconstrained goods. The first-order conditions are:

$$U_i^* - \lambda^* p_i = 0 \quad i = 1, \ldots, k - 1$$

$$U_i^* - \lambda^* p_i - \mu_i = 0 \quad i = k, \ldots, n$$

$$P_L T - \sum_{i=1}^{n} p_i x_i = 0$$

$$b_i - x_i = 0 \quad i = k, \ldots, n$$

Total differentiation yields

$$[M] \begin{bmatrix} dx_j \\ \cdots \\ d\lambda^* \\ \cdots \\ d\mu_t \end{bmatrix} = \begin{bmatrix} \lambda^* \, dp_i \\ \cdots\cdots\cdots\cdots\cdots \\ -P_L \, dT - T \, dp_L + \sum_{i=1}^{n} x_i dp_i \\ \cdots\cdots\cdots\cdots\cdots \\ -db_t \end{bmatrix} \begin{matrix} j = 1, \ldots, n \\ \\ t = k, \ldots, n \end{matrix}$$

and

$$\frac{\delta x_1}{\delta b_n} = \frac{(-1)M_{2n-k+2,1}}{M}$$

where $[M]$ is $[D]$ with additional borders, M is the determinant of $[M]$, and M_{ij} is the cofactor of the ith row and jth column of that determinant. Further manipulation yields

$$\frac{\delta x_1}{\delta b_n} = (-1)^{-k+1} \frac{\begin{vmatrix} U_{12}^* & \cdots & U_{1,k-1}^* & U_{1n}^* & -p_1 \\ \cdots & \cdots & \cdots & \cdots & \cdots \\ U_{k-1,2}^* & \cdots & U_{k-1,k-1}^* & U_{k-1,n}^* & -p_{k-1} \\ -p_2 & \cdots & -p_{k-1} & -p_n & 0 \end{vmatrix}}{\begin{vmatrix} U_{11}^* & \cdots & U_{1,k-1}^* & -p_1 \\ \cdots & \cdots & \cdots & \cdots \\ U_{k-1,1}^* & \cdots & U_{k-1,k-1}^* & -p_{k-1} \\ -p_1 & \cdots & -p_{k-1} & 0 \end{vmatrix}} \quad (4A.1)$$

If the absence or presence of goods $k, \ldots, n-1$ do not affect the sign of $(\delta x_1/\delta p_n)_{U \text{ const}}$ so that one can write

$$
\text{sign} \left[\left(\frac{\delta x_1}{\delta p_n} \right)_{U \text{ const}} \right] = \text{sign } \lambda(-1)^{k+1} \frac{\begin{vmatrix} U_{12} & \cdots & U_{1,k-1} & U_{1n} & -p_1 \\ \cdots\cdots\cdots\cdots\cdots\cdots\cdots\cdots \\ U_{k-1,2} & \cdots & U_{k-1,k-1} & U_{k-1,n} & -p_{k-1} \\ -p_2 & \cdots & -p_{k-1} & -p_n & 0 \end{vmatrix}}{\begin{vmatrix} U_{11} & \cdots & U_{1,k-1} & U_{1n} & -p_1 \\ \cdots\cdots\cdots\cdots\cdots\cdots\cdots\cdots \\ U_{k-1,1} & \cdots & U_{k-1,k-1} & U_{k-1,n} & -p_{k-1} \\ U_{n1} & \cdots & U_{n,k-1} & U_{nn} & -p_n \\ -p_1 & \cdots & -p_{k-1} & -p_n & 0 \end{vmatrix}} \tag{4A.2}
$$

then the results derived in the main text can be generalized to the multiple-constraint case. The denominators in equations (4A.1) and (4A.2) will differ in sign if $U(\cdot)$ is quasi-concave. Thus, for the result presented in the text to hold with multiple constraints, it must be shown that (remembering that the numerators have the same sign if relationships do not change) $(-1)^{-k+1}$ has the same sign as $\lambda(-1)^{-k+1}$. As shown previously, $\lambda > 0$. Therefore, since $(-1)^{-k+1}/(-1)^{k+1} > 0$, the result holds; that is, an increase (decrease) in the amount available of a constrained good decreases (increases) the demand for substitutes and increases (decreases) the demand for complements.

5

The Political Economy of the Disequilibrium Model

Feedback Effects in the Soviet Union

An important concept in the disequilibrium literature is the feedback effect. For example, in chapter 2 the feedback effects of a decrease in the demand for labor on the demand for consumption goods and on the entire economy were examined and found to be deviation-amplifying. This chapter examines the implications of the feedback effects generated by consumer-goods shortages. In particular, the labor supply response and its effects are examined; first in the context of the Soviet economy and then in a fairly general model of a controlled economy.

There are at least three ways in which Soviet labor supply can be decreased in response to shortages. First, the worker can leave the market altogether. In a household with several workers one or more persons might terminate employment (if possible). Second, insofar as the worker can control the length of his work week, he might decrease his hours or days worked per week (for example, by excused or unexcused absences). Third, if the work week is fixed, the worker might reduce his efforts on the job. In other words, he would take some of his increased consumption of leisure in the form of "on-the-job leisure." With a given capital stock this would imply a lower productivity of labor.

The labor supply response to repressed inflation has important feedback implications, especially for the Soviet economy. This can be seen by use of a simple production-possibilities frontier. Let I = producer goods and C = consumer goods (both A^d and B^0). The frontier is drawn in figure 5-1.

A decrease in (voluntary) labor supply will, *ceteris paribus,* shift the frontier inward, from q^1 to q^2, for example. If the authorities are committed to an investment plan fixed in absolute terms, say $I = I^0$, this can have a feedback effect which is deviation-amplifying. For example, assume q^1 is the relevant frontier, and the authorities choose I^0 which implies a shortage of C. Thus labor supply decreases, and the frontier shifts to q^2. If the authorities stick with their decision to produce I^0, this means that C production will decrease still further (from C^1 to C^2 in figure 5-1), thus calling forth more labor supply decreases, production decreases, and so on. (This will be true in the short run where the capital stock is fixed.)

An implication which perhaps should be pointed out is that labor coercion is a predictable consequence of Soviet economic policy. In order to offset the labor disincentives involved in their policy of heavy investment and low produc-

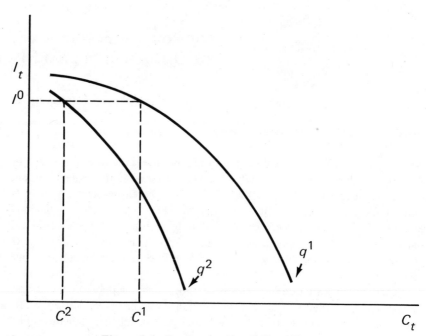

Figure 5-1. Production-Possibilities Frontier.

tion and shortages of consumer goods, the authorities can resort to labor coercion, direction, and so on. A mild form would be moral suasion and pressure, an extreme form labor camps. Thus one can see the practical motive behind the labor market ideology, discussed in chapter 3, that all citizens must work. It is one of the methods used by the authorities to overcome the labor disincentives caused by consumer-goods shortages.[1]

Another feedback effect, which moderates but does not eliminate the above effect, is implied by the institutional processes of the Soviet labor market and the money supply function. As Fearn has argued (see chapter 3), the Soviet authorities have had little actual control over wage expenditures, at least during the period studied here.[2] In figure 5-2 a diagram of the labor market is presented.

The disequilibrium model indicates that consumer-goods shortages result in a decrease in the supply of labor; that is, L^s shifts back to $L^{s'}$. The market is then cleared at a higher real wage w^2. The more vertical the demand for labor function, the higher the new wage will be. In a system emphasizing fulfillment of output plans rather than cost control, one would expect a nearly vertical labor demand. Therefore with a decrease in labor supply there is not much of a change in labor transacted, but there is a considerable increase in the wage rate. Thus a feedback effect of shortages is wage increases which in turn increase the inflationary pressures, since wage increases in the Soviet case imply an increase in the

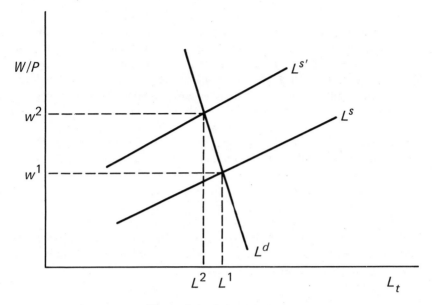

Figure 5-2. Labor Market.

money supply without necessarily any increase in consumer-goods output. The authorities, one way or another, create the funds for wage overexpenditures, and wage overexpenditures amount to an increase in the money supply. Thus the dynamics of the labor market's interaction with the consumer-goods market causes the Soviet authorities to lose some of their control of the wage funds and the money supply.[3] The "wage-push" process can be stopped by restrictions on labor mobility, as was attempted, apparently with some success, in 1938 to 1950.[4]

This analysis of feedback effects is meant to be suggestive only. In particular, no formal analysis aimed at determining whether the processes are finite has been attempted. Such analysis would require a model of policy maker behavior. However, even without such a formal model, one could presume that a policy of labor coercion and/or promises of more consumer goods in the future would dampen these effects—by stopping (one way or another) the backward shifting labor supply depicted in both figures and by forcing or inducing more saving. This subject is pursued further in the next section.

Feedback Effects in a Controlled Economy: The Determination of Saving and Labor Freedom

Much of the discussion of economic policy involves the desirability of government determination of the economy's output mix, including the mix between present and future consumption goods (the saving decision). The purpose of this section is to investigate some of the implications of government determination of the saving decision; in particular, the implications for labor freedom are highlighted. The preceding section discusses the possible effects of the government's choosing an excessively high rate of saving in the context of a disequilibrium model in a controlled economy such as the Soviet Union's. There it is suggested that the government, in order to counteract the decreases in voluntary labor supply induced by its choice of the quantity of consumption goods made available, would probably resort to some combination of labor coercion and promises of more consumption goods in the future. Otherwise, the government's plans for the future might be foiled by the backward shift in labor supply, which would make more difficult the realization of the government's planned amount of saving (investment).

The purpose of this section is to discuss more generally the policy questions raised in the preceding section. In order to do so, the nature of the problem facing the policymakers is presented graphically. Conclusions and implications of the analysis are then discussed.

Consider an economy in which all production is done by the government but where there is a free labor market in the sense that labor can choose how much of its time it wants to sell to the government. The saving decision is made by the government; the household sector merely supplies labor and consumes the one homogeneous good in the economy. The output that is not consumed is invested as an addition to the capital stock. The government hires labor and uses it with capital in order to produce the one good in the economy. The household supplies homogeneous labor in return for the consumption good. Call the one good in the economy Y. If it is consumed, it is C; if it is saved (invested), it is I and is added to the capital stock. Labor L is exchanged for C.

The basic problem facing government policymakers can be put in simple graphical form by just looking at a single period and by assuming that labor is myopic in that it cares about present consumption only. In such a case, three simple relationships describe the economy faced by the government:

$$L = L(C) \tag{5.1}$$

$$Y = C + I \tag{5.2}$$

$$Y = Y(L) \tag{5.3}$$

Equation (5.1) is a labor supply equation similar to the L^s function derived in chapter 4, (5.2) expresses the homogeneity of the good, and (5.3) is the economy's production function with a given capital stock.

Figure 5-3 shows in graphical form the interrelationships among these three equations. In the Northeast quadrant, the labor supply function indicates that the more present consumption is offered, the more labor supply is forthcoming.

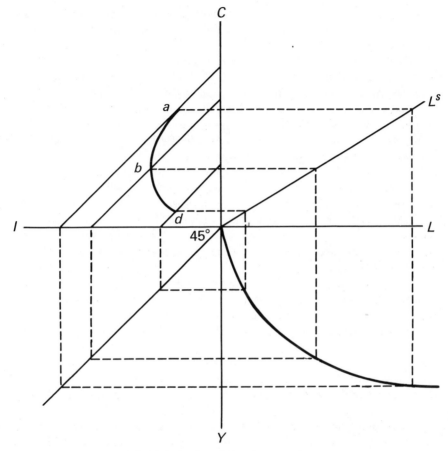

Figure 5-3. Social Equilibrium Curve.

(For simplicity, the labor supply curve is drawn as a straight line through the origin.) In the Southeast quadrant, the usual production relation between labor and output (given the capital stock) is drawn. The Southwest quadrant contains a 45° line that transmits the value on the Y axis onto the I axis. In the Northwest quadrant the homogeneity of good Y is used to show the tradeoff between investment and present consumption. Maximum I is derived from the Y axis, and hence the production function; and the 45° line between the I and C axes shows that an equal amount of investment must be forgone in order to increase present consumption available by a certain amount. The apparatus in figure 5-3 can be used to derive what might be called a "social equilibrium" curve in that it shows the output combinations of C and I consistent with the labor supply and production functions of the economy. The government, when making its saving decision, can choose any point that it would like on the social equilibrium curve without disturbing the household sector (in the sense of forcing it off its supply of labor curve).

The social equilibrium curve is derived as follows. First, an amount of C is posited, and the amount of L forthcoming is read off the labor supply function in the Northeast quadrant. The resulting amount of L is then used, by way of the production function in the Southeast quadrant, to derive an amount of Y, which is then transmitted to the Northwest quadrant via the 45° line in the Southwest quadrant. The 45° line between the I value ($I = Y$) and the C axis amounts to a production-possibilities frontier with the given L from the Northeast quadrant. The original C value is then projected onto the derived production-possibilities frontier; the intersection represents a point of social equilibrium in that the particular (C, I) combination is consistent with the labor supply and production functions. The process is then repeated for different amounts of C. As the reader can verify, the resulting social equilibrium curve will have the shape of the curve *abd* in figure 5-3. (The dashed lines in figure 5-3 are used in constructing *abd*.)

The government faces a problem when its plans for saving (investment) exceed the maximum possible (at, say, point b) on the social equilibrium curve. In such a situation the government has three alternatives: abandon its plans, shift the labor supply function outward, or shift the production function downward. The first alternative is not considered here. The third alternative is what the government is attempting to do (in the longer run) by adopting an ambitious saving/investment plan. The second alternative is the one of interest to us because of the various ways in which the government may try to bring about the desired shift in labor supply. The two ways of shifting the labor supply, and hence the social equilibrium curve, discussed here are labor coercion and campaigns to get the household to work more now for future consumption goods. (Recall that in figure 5-3 the extreme assumption is made that the household sector cares nothing about future consumption goods and hence present saving/investment plans.) It is readily seen that a forced or induced outward shift of the labor supply function in the Northeast quadrant will shift the social equilibrium curve outward and thus improve—from the government's point of view—the menu of choices open to the government.[5]

This section has shown that in an economy where the government is the producer and determines the society's saving/investment decision, the government confronts what is called here a "social equilibrium" relation that limits the government's range of choices for saving or investment. The limit stems from the fact that the household sector is free to cut back its labor supply if the amount of present consumption goods available is not an adequate incentive. That is, labor supply is a positive function of the amount of present consumption goods available. A government that wants to increase present investment may then have to resort either to the exhortation of the benefits of working now for future consumption or to the coercion of labor in the present (or to both). Thus, in an economy in which the government controls production and saving, there is the danger that controls on labor inputs will be resorted to also. In this way, government control of production and saving/investment decisions imperils labor freedom.

The present analysis has shown a connection between governmental controls over production and labor freedom.[6] The connection is not inevitable, according to the analysis presented here, since the government may choose to live with the constraint imposed by the social equilibrium relation. However, the incentive to impose labor coercion is clearly present. Finally, it should be pointed out that even though this study deals with the Soviet Union, the analysis and conclusions of this section are more general.

Notes

1. Similarly, the collective farm market's existence increases at least urban workers' incentives by providing another outlet for excess purchasing power (and thus an alternative to reducing labor supply) and another source of consumer goods. Thus the authorities tolerate it despite its ideological shortcomings.

2. Robert M. Fearn, "Controls over Wage Funds and Inflationary Pressures in the U.S.S.R."

3. This analysis requires the labor market to exhibit Walrasian stability, that is, $\delta L^s/\delta w > \delta L^d/\delta w$.

4. Franklyn D. Holzman, "Soviet Inflationary Pressures, 1928-1957: Causes and Cures," pp. 181-87. It is interesting how similar the situation was to that described by Domar in his analysis of serfdom under the tsars. See Evsey D. Domar, "The Causes of Slavery or Serfdom: A Hypothesis."

5. The apparatus developed in figure 5-3 would appear applicable to other policy decisions as well, for example, the determination of a social equilibrium between taxes and disposable income.

6. Other aspects of the connection between economic controls and freedom are discussed by F.A. Hayek, *The Road to Serfdom* and *The Constitution of Liberty,* and Milton Friedman, *Capitalism and Freedom.*

6 Data

Sources, Methodology, and Quality

Although the years of Stalin's rule were years of disequilibrium, the formal empirical work of this book is confined to post-Stalin years. This is mainly because the data for the Stalin years are unreliable and not extensively published. The period tested formally here is 1955 to 1967. This section presents the raw data used and a discussion of the sources and methodology involved in obtaining them. In addition, the quality of the data is discussed. The deficiencies of Soviet data are legendary, and the discussion therefore focuses on the quality of data taken directly from Soviet sources, especially the price and sales indexes. Except for a few comments, the discussion does not deal with data obtained from Western sources. The interested reader can go to the source itself for a discussion of data quality, methodology, and so on.

Table 6-1 contains price variables. The calculation of the average monthly wage is mostly from Soviet sources. The main source is *Trud* v *SSSR* (1968) which has been found to be relatively reliable.[1]

The consumer price index, taken from Bronson and Severin, is only as good as its component parts, the official price indexes of state retail and collective farm market (CFM) sales. The reservations about them also apply to this index.

The quality of the official price indexes for state and cooperative retail sales and collective farm market sales merits comment. A detailed description of how the latter is constructed is presented by Bornstein.[2] Bornstein presents several criticisms of the CFM indexes, mostly having to do with data collection procedures, aggregation methods, and sampling techniques. He concludes that the CFM price and quantity indexes are subject to a large amount of error, that the sales indexes are more reliable than the price indexes, and that, in general, the wider the coverage of an index, the less reliable it is.[3] Schroeder briefly reiterates the criticisms presented by Bornstein and states that "the published price index may understate price changes over time...."[4]

Thus the series on prices and sales on the collective farm market are, at best, only rough estimates. The extrarural index (that is, all cities and rural localities) is used because this book is concerned with the total economy, not just the urban sector. For this increase in coverage a price must be paid. In this case the price is a decrease in realiability and the inclusion of sales to cooperatives in the data. Possible double-counting of these sales is not of concern since measuring consumption is not the purpose of this book. The only concern is whether

Table 6-1
Wage and Price Data

Year	Official State Retail Price Index[a]	Official CFM Price Index[b]	Consumer Price Index[c]	Average Monthly Wage (Rubles) of Nonprivate Civilian Employees[d]
1955	100.0	100.0	100.0	54.6
1956	100.0	90.7	98.8	56.4
1957	100.0	87.9	98.4	59.1
1958	102.2	91.6	101.0	61.5
1959	101.4	89.7	100.1	62.6
1960	100.7	90.7	99.6	65.0
1961	100.0	95.3	99.7	69.6
1962	101.4	102.8	101.7	73.5
1963	102.2	107.5	102.9	75.5
1964	102.2	110.3	103.3	79.1
1965	101.4	101.9	101.6	85.4
1966	100.7	97.2	100.4	89.9
1967	100.7	97.2	100.4	94.0

[a]Computed from *Nar. Khoz. 1960*, p. 716; *1959*, p. 677; *1965*, p. 652; *1962*, p. 532; *1922-1972*, p. 409; *1963*, p. 539; *1967*, p. 739.

[b]Computed from *Nar. Khoz. 1960*, p. 736; *1959*, p. 708; *1964*, p. 657; *1961*, p. 664; *1968*, p. 654; *1962*, p. 541; *1965*, p. 665.

[c]Computed from D. Bronson and B. Severin, "Recent Trends in Consumption and Disposable Money Income in the U.S.S.R.," p. 526; "Soviet Consumer Welfare: The Brezhnev Era," p. 393. Their index uses 1955 weights to combine the reported state retail price index with the reported collective farm market price index.

[d]See appendix 6A.

inclusion of these sales to cooperatives biases the measure of changes in collective farm market sales and prices. This depends on whether these sales have behaved in a significantly different manner from CFM sales to the population. There is no evidence that they have.

Bornstein also presents a detailed discussion of state and cooperative retail prices. According to Bornstein, the prices used to construct the official price indexes are taken from official price lists. However, the indexes do not reflect changes in prices brought about by such things as the introduction of "new" products, and it is often the case that a "new" product will be introduced that hardly differs at all from the "old" product in order to increase prices, the value of sales, and so on. In some cases, Bornstein contends, the "new" products are actually of lower quality. Thus the official price indexes understate inflation; and when one of these indexes is used to deflate nominal retail sales—recorded at the actual, that is, higher, prices—the level of real sales is overstated. According to Bornstein, official price indexes are used to convert nominal sales to real sales.

Thus, official data on real growth in retail sales are biased upward.[5] One of Bornstein's conclusions is that the official retail price index "fails to reflect properly the movement in the price level . . . because of the various types of price changes which it omits."[6]

For the purposes of this book the most disturbing point Bornstein makes is that the price index does not properly reflect changes in prices actually paid by consumers for retail goods. Essentially, the index just reflects prices on official state price lists. Many other Western economists, and indeed some Russian economists as well, have also made this point.[7] In reference to the omission of new prices on "new" goods, Schroeder quotes a Soviet source who confirms that the introduction of such goods may be a source of hidden price inflation. Schroeder goes on to point out that "revised prices on products arbitrarily designated as 'new' or 'improved' could be easily linked into the chain index with . . . zero effect on the measured index of prices between Period 1 and Period 2." She also makes the point that the official index is not an index of actual prices paid by the consumer and that there is "considerable evidence of what may be fairly widespread violation of state retail prices by the stores."[8]

What are the implications of this? One is that the official series does not reflect what Schroeder suspects to have been "considerable hidden price inflation," especially in the 1960s.[9] Bush corroborates this suspicion that actual prices paid by consumers on the state retail market have crept upward rather than remaining essentially constant as implied by the official price index.[10] This has potentially serious consequences for the present analysis if the official index is used.

One possible way around this difficulty is to construct a retail price index. However the necessary data are not readily available.[11] Another way is to ignore it and just use the official index anyway.[12] Still another way is to estimate the actual price level and hence the amount of hidden inflation. In the next section such an estimate is derived. First, evidence of the hidden inflation is presented. Then the actual price level is estimated. Finally, estimates of the general price level and real sales on the state and cooperative retail market are also obtained. The result is a price-level series showing the (estimated) amount of hidden inflation in the Soviet Union and a real sales series corrected for the overstatement introduced by the use of a faulty price deflator.

Table 6-2 contains various quantity variables. The data on savings deposits are of fairly high quality. As Powell states, "Of all conceivable areas of monetary statistics, the Soviet authorities have probably released more nearly comprehensive and detailed data on savings bank deposits than on any other. . . ."[13] The problem with this variable is that it does not capture all savings by Soviet households. State bank deposits are omitted because data are not available for 1955–1957. However, this is an insignificant omission since the level of these deposits is small and has not varied much (for example, 120 million rubles in 1958 and 128 million rubles in 1967).[14] Bond purchases are deliberately omitted because early in the period of study they were a form of taxation rather than voluntary

Table 6-2
Sales and Savings Data

Year	State and Cooperative Retail Sales[a] Index (in Constant Prices)[b]	Personal Services (Million 1968 Rubles)[c]	State and Cooperative Retail Sales[a] (Million Current Rubles)[d]	CFM Sales Index (in Constant Prices)[e]	Total Savings Bank Deposits at End of Year (Million Current Rubles)[f]
1954					4,835
1955	100.0	6,754	50,194	100.0	5,366
1956	108.7	7,209	54,743	101.8	6,375
1957	124.0	7,783	62,501	102.4	8,058
1958	131.7	8,403	67,720	101.2	8,719
1959	142.3	9,076	71,923	99.4	10,056
1960	156.7	9,823	78,555	92.2	10,909
1961	162.5	10,485	81,076	93.4	11,671
1962	172.6	11,330	87,296	91.6	12,745
1963	180.8	12,005	91,685	83.2	13,992
1964	190.4	12,905	96,361	83.8	15,707
1965	209.1	13,918	104,762	87.4	18,727
1966	227.4	15,011	113,015	94.0	22,915
1967	248.6	16,275	123,579	98.2	26,869

[a]Including public catering.

[b]Computed from *Nar. Khoz. 1959*, p. 633; *1964*, p. 623; *1961*, p. 630; *1922-1972*, p. 389.

[c]See appendix 6B.

[d]*Nar. Khoz. 1961*, p. 633; *1922-1972*, p. 391.

[e]Computed from *Nar. Khoz. 1960*, p. 736; *1959*, p. 708; *1964*, p. 657; *1961*, p. 664; *1968*, p. 654; *1962*, p. 541; *1965*, p. 665.

[f]*Nar. Khoz. 1956*, p. 282; *1960*, p. 854; *1959*, p. 810; *1964*, p. 595; *1962*, p. 492; *1963*, p. 509; *1965*, p. 600; *1922-1972*, p. 373.

savings, and later, when they became voluntary, purchases fell to a low level. Estimating the amount of voluntary purchases during the period of compulsory purchases is virtually impossible, and so they are omitted altogether. The major potential problem with the savings variable is that it omits currency in the hands of the households. Currency hoarding is, of course, a substitute for savings deposits. Various estimates of currency in circulation after 1937 are reported for a few years by Powell,[15] but it would seem safer to neglect currency on the assumption that the relationship between hoarding and deposits did not change during the period, a view taken by Bronson and Severin.[16]

The indexes of sales volume on the state and cooperative retail market and the collective farm market also merit discussion. In a recent study of Soviet sales statistics, Goldman points out that the official retail sales data include sales that are not strictly speaking retail sales.[17] There is no evidence that the proportion of sales not involving the consumer has changed significantly over time. Because concern here is not with absolute levels of consumption, but rather with changes in levels and subsequent effects of these changes on market behavior, Goldman's reservations do not pose an important problem.

Another, potentially more serious, problem is "the fact that the definition of what is included as retail sales is subject to periodic change."[18] However, there seem to have been no major changes during the 1955-1967 period, so the problem is not a serious one for this book. Another problem, according to Goldman, is that collective farm market sales are not adequately covered, especially with regard to informal transactions.[19] This is discussed later.

A main problem with these sales statistics is that they are not a measure of consumption because of the many omissions. However, this is irrelevant for our purpose which is not concerned with consumption per se, but rather with sales on markets. Unfortunately, there are also many omissions of market sales, the most prominent example being services. An attempt has been made to correct for this omission in an alternative calculation (see appendix 6B) which includes many services, housing among them. Another omission is private transactions—legal, semilegal, and illegal. These are not reported in any complete or systematic fashion. A major shortcoming of the empirical work in this book is the exclusion of this important spillover effect. However, it is difficult to see what can be done about it, given the absence of any data.

A final problem is the method by which the data are converted to real terms. The official Soviet indexes of state and cooperative retail sales and collective farm market sales (columns 1 and 4 of table 6-2) are supposedly deflated by official price indexes.[20] In the former case this causes a problem of overstatement of sales because of the hidden inflation in the price index. The nominal sales series obviously avoids this since it is not deflated.

Table 6-3 presents certain labor and population data. These are from reliable Western sources. Tables 6-4 and 6-5 contain variables used to complete the simultaneous-equations system. Total utilized net material product is constructed from a Western source. The binary variables are explained in appendixes 6D and 6E. No particular problems are involved in these data except that total utilized net material product (NMP) excludes many services. (NMP is used as a determinant of the demand for labor, and hence services output should be included also. However, NMP is a reasonable proxy for total output for its very limited purpose in this book since NMP and services output are positively related.) Becker found that the NMP data that he obtained from Soviet sources are more reliable than such data used to be.[21]

Two alternative capital stock series are presented in table 6-5. The capital series does not play an important role in the empirical tests (its role is similar to that of NMP), and so it does not merit extensive discussion. The data used are the best available without doing extensive research in Soviet sources and, in effect, duplicating Moorsteen and Powell's study for each year in the study period.[22] No known biases exist in the data although they are, of course, subject to the usual problems of Soviet data. In terms of what should be regarded as the

Table 6-3
Labor and Population Data
(thousands)

Year	Average Nonprivate Civilian Employment[a]	Average Civilian Employment[b]	Population, Ages 16 to 59 for Men, 16 to 54 for Women (Working-Age Population)[b]	Total Population[c]
1955	75,051	87,642	114,658	196,159
1956	77,569	90,383	116,873	199,658
1957	78,760	91,496	118,639	203,170
1958	80,905	93,702	119,574	206,806
1959	82,367	94,047	119,606	210,529
1960	84,332	95,398	110,459	214,329
1961	86,561	97,968	119,622	218,145
1962	88,300	99,727	120,233	221,730
1963	89,926	100,905	121,245	225,063
1964	92,458	103,465	122,586	228,149
1965	95,815	107,929	124,142	230,936
1966	98,309	110,669	125,681	233,533
1967	100,674	112,636	127,183	235,994

[a]See appendix 6A.
[b]H. Feshbach and S. Rapawy, "Labor Constraints in the Five-Year Plan," pp. 520–21.
[c]F. Leedy, "Demographic Trends in the U.S.S.R.," p. 472.

Table 6-4
Net Material Product and Binary Variables

Year	Total Utilized Net Material Product (Million 1955 Rubles)[a]	Weather[b,c]	Government Policy toward Private Agriculture[d,e]
1955	97,600	0	0
1956	106,230	0	0
1957	112,321	0	0
1958	128,220	0	1
1959	135,579	1	1
1960	147,360	0	1
1961	157,864	0	1
1962	166,785	0	1
1963	173,248	1	1
1964	190,426	0	1
1965	202,294	1	0
1966	218,909	0	0
1967	236,703	0	0

[a]See appendix 6C.
[b]This binary variable takes the value 1 for bad weather and 0 otherwise.
[c]See appendix 6D.
[d]This binary variable takes the value 1 for a hostile policy and 0 otherwise.
[e]See appendix 6E.

Table 6–5
Capital Stock Data
(million 1955 rubles, on January 1)

Year	Nonresidential and Working Capital[a]	Total Capital Stock
1955	175,880	199,201
1956	196,980	224,301
1957	221,727	253,574
1958	242,519	280,264
1959	269,135	315,280
1960	296,179	351,597
1961	325,703	391,045
1962	360,412	435,895
1963	396,129	482,081
1964	428,926	526,122
1965	470,889	578,365
1966	513,153	631,672
1967	559,679	689,777

Source: See appendix 6F.

[a]Approximate; see discussion in appendix 6F.

relevant capital stock in the demand for labor, the two concepts presented in the table are used to test the sensitivity of the empirical results to different concepts of the capital stock.

Estimates of the Hidden Inflation in the Soviet Union

Table 6–6 presents the percentage change between 1955 and 1967 of the official state and cooperative real retail sales index and a Western estimate of real consumption. One immediately notices the difference between the change in the Soviet index of state and cooperative sales and Bronson and Severin's measure of consumption. The difference could be due to the different coverages involved. Bronson and Severin's estimate covers total consumption including "free" gov-

Table 6–6
Changes in Sales and Consumption

	Percentage Change from 1955 to 1967
State and cooperative real retail sales (index)	149[a]
Real consumption	87[b]

[a]From Table 6–2.
[b]From D. Bronson and B. Severin, "Soviet Consumer Welfare," pp. 398–401.

Table 6-7
Components of Consumption, Western Estimates
(million constant rubles)

Component	1955	1967	Percentage Change
Food	63,535	107,848	70
Soft goods	17,120	33,034	93
Consumer durables	2,062	8,259	301
Personal services	6,754	16,275	141
Health and education	9,255	19,566	111

Source: D. Bronson and B. Severin, "Soviet Consumer Welfare," pp. 398–401.

ernment services, collective farm market goods, home-produced goods, and housing. The official index covers only retail sales (including public catering) on state and cooperative markets.

However, not all the difference can be attributed to different coverages. To investigate this, the components of Bronson and Severin's index are presented in table 6-7. The official index does not include the items in the last two rows, so attention can be focused on the first three items. (Notice that the percentage changes in personal services and health and education are large enough to indicate that they are not the major source of any difference between the Soviet and Bronson and Severin figures.) The Soviet Union publishes indexes on food and nonfood sales in state and cooperative stores. The percentage changes in these are as follows: food, 138; nonfood, 161.[23] Bronson and Severin's food category contains state and cooperative sales, CFM sales, and home-produced food. CFM sales changed by a –2 percent. By making the not too unreasonable assumption that home-produced food declined by the same percentage,[24] it is possible to lump the two together and calculate what weight for combined CFM sales and home-produced food is necessary in order to reconcile the official estimate of state and cooperative food sales with Bronson and Severin's estimate of food consumption. It turns out that the weight must be about one-half; that is, about half of the food consumption must consist of CFM purchases and home-produced items.[25] The share of food consumption deriving from CFM purchases and home-produced food in 1955 was 0.50.[26] Since this share has been falling since 1955,[27] the official sales index probably overstates growth in sales, probably because of hidden inflation that inflated sales in current prices but which was not picked up in the price index used to deflate sales. Other explanations are possible (for example, differing changes in CFM sales and home-produced goods), so the conclusion here is tentative.

For simplicity and with little loss of realism it can be assumed that all soft goods and consumer durables in Bronson and Severin's data are sold through the state and cooperative retail network and that all nonfood sales in the official index consist of these soft goods and consumer durables. By combining rows 2 and 3 of table 6-7, a percentage change can be obtained for comparison with the change in the Soviet nonfood index. The combined percentage change is 115, less than the Soviet index change. The conclusion is straightforward: The Soviet index overstates growth in real sales. Again, this result is probably due to the failure of the price deflator to reflect the hidden inflation that took place between 1955 and 1967.[28] Thus, the difference between the percentage changes in the official retail sales index and Bronson and Severin's consumption measure is probably attributable partly to different coverages and partly to the fact that the index overstates increases in real sales. The most likely explanation of this overstatement is the existence of hidden inflation (thus confirming the suspicions of many Western scholars).[29]

The kind of information presented earlier can be used to estimate the hidden inflation on the state and cooperative retail markets in the following manner. Define the price index of these goods to be p_t^a/p_1^a where a stands for actual and the subscript denotes time period. X_t is the quantity of goods sold (treating all goods as one good). Thus,

$$\frac{p_t^a X_t}{p_t^a} p_1^a = p_1^a X_t = \text{real value of sales}$$

The percentage change in real sales is given by

$$\frac{(p_t^a X_t / p_t^a) p_1^a - (p_1^a X_1 / p_1^a) p_1^a}{(p_1^a X_1 / p_1^a) p_1^a} = \frac{p_1^a X_t - p_1^a X_1}{p_1^a X_1}$$

$$= \frac{X_t - X_1}{X_1}$$

This is what the Bronson and Severin figures are supposed to measure.[30] The Soviet figures do not measure this because the price index used is p_t^*/p_1^*, where the asterisk indicates some official's conception of what prices are. Thus,

$$\frac{p_t^a X_t}{p_t^*} p_1^* = \text{official estimate of real value of sales}$$

The official percentage change in real sales is, then,

$$\frac{(p_t^a X_t / p_t^*) p_1^* - (p_1^a X_1 / p_1^*) p_1^*}{(p_1^a X_1 / p_1^*) p_1^*} = \frac{p_t^a X_t p_1^*}{p_t^* p_1^a X_1} - 1$$

Thus the difference between the official estimate of percentage change and the Bronson and Severin estimate is

$$\Delta_t = \frac{p_t^a X_t \, p_1^*}{p_t^* p_1^a X_1} - \frac{p_1^a X_t}{p_1^a X_1}$$

All these are observable except p_t^a and p_1^a. Setting $p_1^a = 100$, one can solve for p_t^a in each of the following years (in this case, 1956 to 1967). To do so, the official nonfood retail price index (from table 6G-1) is used for p^*, Bronson and Severin's series (in index form) of consumer durables and soft goods is used for X (and is presented in table 6-8), and this series and the official nonfood sales index (also presented in table 6-8) are used to calculate Δ. The formula for calculating p_t^a is

$$p_t^a = \frac{p_t^*(100\Delta_t + X_t)}{X_t} \qquad (6.1)$$

Using these data, the p_t^a are solved for; that is, estimates of an actual price index for nonfood items sold on state and cooperative retail markets are obtained. These estimates are presented in column 1 of table 6-9. Assuming that

Table 6-8
Real Sales Indexes

Year	Consumer Durables and Soft Goods[a]	Official Nonfood Sales Index[b]	Difference in Percentage Change over 1955 (100Δ)[c]
1955	100.0	100.0	
1956	106.5	109.9	3.4
1957	116.8	127.8	11.0
1958	125.7	136.5	10.8
1959	136.2	148.3	12.1
1960	148.2	165.0	16.8
1961	153.4	168.4	15.0
1962	159.7	179.1	19.4
1963	162.1	183.3	21.2
1964	168.4	192.0	23.6
1965	181.6	215.6	34.0
1966	198.1	236.5	38.4
1967	215.3	261.2	45.9

[a]Calculated from D. Bronson and B. Severin, "Soviet Consumer Welfare," pp. 398–401.
[b]Calculated from *Nar. Khoz. 1922-1972*, p. 389; *1961*, p. 630; *1964*, p. 622; *1972*, p. 574.
[c]Calculated from columns 1 and 2.

Table 6-9
Estimates of Price Indexes

Year	Estimated State Nonfood Retail Price Index[a]	Official State Food Retail Price Index[b]	State Retail Price Index	
			Maximum Estimate[c]	Minimum Estimate[d]
1955	100.0	100.0	100.0	100.0
1956	102.5	101.4	102.5	101.9
1957	108.7	101.4	108.7	104.8
1958	107.8	105.7	107.8	106.7
1959	107.3	105.0	107.3	106.1
1960	108.0	104.3	108.0	106.0
1961	105.7	103.5	105.7	104.5
1962	108.0	106.4	108.0	107.2
1963	108.9	108.5	108.9	108.7
1964	108.9	107.8	108.9	108.3
1965	111.6	107.8	111.6	109.6
1966	110.4	107.1	110.4	108.7
1967	112.2	107.1	112.2	109.5

[a]Calculated from tables 6-8 and 6G-1 using (6.1).
[b]From table 6G-1.
[c]Calculated from column 1 of this table, assuming that actual inflation in food prices is equal to that estimated for nonfood prices.
[d]Calculated from columns 1 and 2 of this table using the weights 0.53 for food prices and 0.47 for nonfood prices. (These weights are the average of those implied by the data in columns 1 to 3 of table 6G-1.)

the hidden inflation in food is equal to that in durables and soft goods, an estimate of the actual price index in state retail trade can be obtained. This is presented in column 3 of table 6-9. By assumption the entries in this column are the same as those in the first column. However, this estimate of the overall state retail price index probably overstates the total hidden inflation rate since it is easier to invent "new" or "improved" products in the durables and soft-goods sectors than in the food sector. Thus column 3 represents a maximum estimate of the price level in the state and cooperative retail markets. A minimum estimate of the price level can be obtained by assuming that there was no hidden inflation in the food sector. The official series on prices in the state food sector is used as published. Combining this series with that of column 1 in table 6-9 yields the minimum estimates presented in column 4 of the same table. The estimates of the state retail price index presented in table 6-9 can be used to compute minimum and maximum estimates of the general index of prices paid by consumers, and to deflate a nominal series on state and cooperative retail sales in order to obtain minimum and maximum estimates of a real sales index on state and cooperative retail markets. These estimates are presented in table 6-10

Table 6-10
Certain Data Reflecting Estimated Actual Prices

| Year | General Consumer Price Index | | Real Sales Index on Official Retail Market | |
	Maximum Estimate[a]	Minimum Estimate[a]	Maximum Estimate[b]	Minimum Estimate[b]
1955	100.0	100.0	100.0	100.0
1956	101.5	100.9	107.0	106.4
1957	106.9	103.3	118.8	114.6
1958	106.4	105.4	126.4	125.2
1959	105.8	104.7	135.1	133.5
1960	106.5	104.7	147.6	144.9
1961	104.8	103.7	154.6	152.8
1962	107.5	106.8	162.2	161.0
1963	108.8	108.6	168.0	167.7
1964	109.0	108.5	177.3	176.3
1965	110.8	108.9	190.4	187.0
1966	109.3	107.7	207.1	203.9
1967	110.9	108.4	224.8	219.4

[a]Calculated according to the formula used in D. Bronson and B. Severin, "Soviet Consumer Welfare," p. 396, that is, $p = (91.3 \cdot$ state retail price index $+ 8.7 \cdot$ CFM price index)/ 100. The first index in the formula is from columns 3 and 4 of table 6-9, the second from column 2 of table 6-1.

[b]Calculated from column 3 of table 6-2 using columns 4 and 3 of table 6-9.

along with the exact methodology used. Columns 1 and 2 are, of course, estimates of the actual consumer price level in the Soviet Union.

The problem of quality change creates a potential problem for the interpretation of the estimated hidden price inflation. If improvements in quality are significant, the estimate will tend to overstate the true amount of inflation. However, as mentioned earlier, it can also be the case that the new goods with higher prices are actually of lower quality; such phenomena will mean that any estimate will tend to understate inflation. The net effect of both of these quality-change problems is indeterminate.

The estimates presented here are rough, but they allow one to make some conclusions about the extent of hidden inflation in the Soviet Union and its effect on certain official Soviet data. Comparisons between official data and present estimates can be easily made through use of table 6-11. Thus there has been more price inflation in the Soviet Union than is indicated by official price indexes. Furthermore, real sales on the state and cooperative retail market have not increased as much as is indicated by the official sales index. However, the price inflation has been mild (average annual rate is 0.8 to 1.2 percent), particularly relative to recent Western experience, and the increase in retail sales is considerable.

Table 6-11
Comparisons of Official and Estimated Data

Year	State Retail Price Index			General Consumer Price Index			Real Sales Index on State and Cooperative Retail Market		
	Official[a]	Minimum Estimate[b]	Maximum Estimate[b]	Official[a]	Minimum Estimate[c]	Maximum Estimate[c]	Official[d]	Minimum Estimate[c]	Maximum Estimate[c]
1955	100.0	100.0	100.0	100.0	100.0	100.0	100.0	100.0	100.0
1956	100.0	101.9	102.5	98.8	100.9	101.5	108.7	106.4	107.0
1957	100.0	104.8	108.7	98.4	103.3	106.9	124.0	114.6	118.8
1958	102.2	106.7	107.8	101.0	105.4	106.4	131.7	125.2	126.4
1959	101.4	106.1	107.3	100.1	104.7	105.8	142.3	133.5	135.1
1960	100.7	106.0	108.0	99.6	104.7	106.5	156.7	144.9	147.6
1961	100.0	104.5	105.7	99.7	103.7	104.8	162.5	152.8	154.6
1962	101.4	107.2	108.0	101.7	106.8	107.5	172.6	161.0	162.2
1963	102.2	108.7	108.9	102.9	108.6	108.8	180.8	167.7	168.0
1964	102.2	108.3	108.9	103.3	108.5	109.0	190.4	176.3	177.3
1965	101.4	109.6	111.6	101.6	108.9	110.8	209.1	187.0	190.4
1966	100.7	108.7	110.4	100.4	107.7	109.3	227.4	203.9	207.1
1967	100.7	109.5	112.2	100.4	108.4	110.9	248.6	219.4	224.8

[a]From table 6-1.
[b]From table 6-9.
[c]From table 6-10.
[d]From table 6-2.

The rate of inflation is misleading in one respect since there has been repressed inflation in the Soviet Union during this period as well. What the results of this section show is that not all the inflationary pressures have been repressed. The pressures have resulted in some actual inflation, although most of it has been hidden from the official price index.

Specification

This section describes how the data in the first two sections of this chapter are used to compute the data needed to test the hypotheses embodied in the equation system of chapter 4.

The four prices W, P^B, P^A, and P are the monthly wage of nonprivate civilian employees, the estimated retail price index, the CFM price index, and the estimated consumer price index, respectively, of tables 6-1, 6-9, and 6-10. In order to correct for population changes and shifts in its distribution by age, certain variables are divided by the working-age population (from table 6-3). The estimated state and cooperative retail sales and the CFM sales indexes (tables 6-10 and 6-2) are adjusted in this way in order to get B^0 and A^d, respectively. The value of s^d is calculated by first taking the differences between two years in total savings deposits (table 6-2). The differences are then divided by working-age population and then by P. H_{-1} is set equal to the level of savings deposits at the end of the previous year; the series is then divided by P and working-age population to get H_{-1}/P. L^s equals nonprivate civilian employment divided by working-age population. Q^0, R, and G are NMP (divided by working-age population) and the two binary variables of table 6-4, respectively. The measures of K^0 are from table 6-5 after dividing by working-age population; the main specification of K^0 is the total capital stock.

An apparent problem results from the use of the data on state and cooperative retail sales as the measure of constrained consumer goods (or the quantity constraint). These data include figures for goods that are not in excess demand. The use of sales, not production, alleviates this by eliminating inventory buildups. It can be shown that using total sales of a group of goods as a constrained good is valid even if some of those goods are not in excess demand. Let x_i represent volume of sales of good, i, x_i^d represent demand for it, and p_i be its price. If the good is in excess demand, then

$$p_i x_i < p_i x_i^d$$

if not, then by the principle of free consumer choice

$$p_i x_i = p_i x_i^d$$

that is, the household need never purchase more than it wants. If there are m goods in the group, then

$$p_i x_i \leqslant p_i x_i^d \quad i = 1, \ldots, m$$

If there is just one good in the group for which there is a shortage, then

$$\sum_{i=1}^{m} p_i x_i < \sum_{i=1}^{m} p_i x_i^d$$

Thus, use of

$$\sum_{i=1}^{m} p_i x_i$$

as the quantity constraint is valid, since the sum is less than the value of total demand for that group of goods. The group as a whole, then, can be viewed as a constrained consumer good even though consumption of some goods in the group is not constrained. However, there will be spillovers into other goods in the group as well as goods outside the group, and at some point there is a danger that most of the spillover effects will take place within the group.

General Movement of the Data

Before moving on to the empirical testing, it is interesting to examine briefly the overall movement of some of the data during the 1955-1967 period. Table 6-12 presents the percentage change between 1955 and 1967 of the indicated variables.

Most noteworthy in a comparison of rows 1 and 4 in table 6-12 is the difference between the changes in the estimated data on state and cooperative sales and Bronson and Severin's on consumption. The difference is mainly due to the different coverages involved. Bronson and Severin's estimate covers total consumption, and the estimate of state and cooperative retail sales (B^0) in table 6-12 (row 1) covers only one (major) component of total consumption. With the exception of housing, B^0 includes all important items in excess demand and sold by the state at a positive price.[31] Hence for purposes of investigating quantity-constrained market behavior and repressed inflation, B^0 is the more appropriate, particularly (since B^0 is a policy variable) in view of the interest in policy implications.

Table 6-12

Changes in Sales and Consumption

	Percentage Change from 1955 to 1967
Estimated state and cooperative real sales per working-age person[a]	98-103
Real personal services per working-age person[a]	117
CFM real sales (index) per working-age person[a]	-11
Western estimate of real consumption per working-age person[b]	69

[a]From tables 6-2, 6-3, and 6-10.

[b]From D. Bronson and B. Severin, "Soviet Consumer Welfare," pp. 398-401, and table 6-3.

Notes

1. Gertrude E. Schroeder, "An Appraisal of Soviet Wage and Income Statistics," p. 294.

2. Morris Bornstein, "Soviet Price Statistics," pp. 379-81.

3. Ibid., pp. 382-83.

4. Schroeder, "Appraisal," p. 311. The origin of these criticisms in Western literature is Jerzy Karcz, "Quantitative Analysis of the Collective Farm Market."

5. Bornstein, "Soviet Price Statistics," pp. 371-73.

6. Ibid., p. 378.

7. See, for example, Marshall I. Goldman, "Consumption Statistics," pp. 338-39.

8. Schroeder, "Appraisal," pp. 309-10.

9. Ibid., p. 313.

10. Keith Bush, "Soviet Inflation," p. 99.

11. Schroeder, "Appraisal," p. 311.

12. This is essentially what Bronson and Severin do in their two studies when they use the official indexes to construct a consumer price index. See David W. Bronson and Barbara S. Severin, "Recent Trends in Consumption and Disposable Money Income in the U.S.S.R." and "Soviet Consumer Welfare."

13. Raymond P. Powell, "Monetary Statistics," pp. 427-28.

14. *Nar. Khoz. 1964,* p. 595; *1968,* p. 597.

15. Powell, "Monetary Statistics," pp. 414-16.

16. Bronson and Severin, "Recent Trends," p. 515.

17. Goldman, "Consumption Statistics," p. 335.

18. Ibid., p. 336.

19. Ibid.

20. Bornstein, "Soviet Price Statistics," p. 373.

21. Abraham S. Becker, "National Income Accounting in the U.S.S.R.," pp. 95–115.

22. Richard Moorsteen and Powell, *The Soviet Capital Stock, 1928–1962.*

23. *Nar. Khoz. 1968,* p. 610.

24. A decline did take place (see Bronson and Severin, "Soviet Consumer Welfare: The Brezhnev Era," p. 383), although its magnitude is uncertain. Negative 2 percent is assumed for simplicity and to avoid the problem of weighting the components.

25. The method used is as follows:
[percentage change in food (state sales)] (x) + (percentage change in CFM and home-produced food) $(1 - x)$ = percentage change in food (Bronson and Severin), where x is the unknown weight of state sales. Solving yields $(138)x + (-2)(1 - x) = 70; x = 0.51$. That is, the necessary weight is 0.49.

26. Computed from data in Central Intelligence Agency, "A Comparison of Consumption in the U.S.S.R. and the U.S.," pp. 12, 102.

27. See Bronson and Severin, "Soviet Consumer Welfare," p. 383.

28. However, the decline in the amount of home-produced clothing (see ibid., p. 384) could account for some of it.

29. Bronson and Severin use some price indexes to calculate their estimates (ibid., p. 397), so their data may also be overstated.

30. The Bronson and Severin series is an estimate of real consumption in the Soviet Union. To construct it, they use data on production, deflated retail sales, and per capita consumption (ibid., p. 402). In this section the Bronson and Severin data on real consumption are used in conjunction with various Soviet indexes to construct a better alternative to the official Soviet price index.

31. The series on personal services (see appendix 6B) includes housing. The percentage change in this series is presented in the second row of table 6-12.

Appendix 6A

Average monthly wages in the national economy are from *Trud v SSSR* (1968), pp. 138–39, for 1955 and 1960–1967; *Nar. Khoz. 1964,* p. 555, for 1958; and the 1956–1957 and 1959 figures are interpolated. Average monthly wages in collective farms are taken from Bronson and Krueger.[1] Numbers of workers and employees (in national economy) and collective farmers are from Feshbach and Rapawy.[2] The sum of these equals average civilian employment (excluding private agriculture and artisans) and is presented in column 1 of table 6-3. Next, the data on workers and employees and collective farmers are used to weight the wage data. The resulting total wages paid is then divided by nonprivate civilian employment to get average monthly wage paid to nonprivate civilian employees and is presented in column 4 of table 6-1.

Notes

1. David W. Bronson and Constance B. Krueger, "The Revolution in Soviet Farm Household Income, 1953–1967," p. 247.

2. Murray Feshbach and Stephen Rapawy, "Labor Constraints in the Five-Year Plan," pp. 520–21. They state that

> Annual average civilian employment refers to the annual average registered number of persons. . . . For the state sector, it is derived as the average of 12 monthly averages which are, in turn, the averages of the daily numbers of persons listed on the rolls of the employing enterprise. A person appears on the rolls of his employing enterprise if he is paid by it; he remains on the rolls during excused absences from work, holidays, etc. For the collective farm sector, the annual average is derived as the average of 12 monthly numbers of participants.

Appendix 6B

The data on personal services include housing and are from Bronson and Severin, "Soviet Consumer Welfare," pp. 398–401. Their measure of housing is based on the "stock of housing (living space) priced at the official average rent per square meter."

Appendix 6C

Price deflators are obtained as follows. The 1958–1965 and 1967 values are taken directly from Becker.[1] The 1966 value is the mean of the two deflators given by Becker. The 1955–1957 values are established by an equation (fitted by least squares on the 1958–1967 data) relating the deflator to time because inspection reveals a time trend in the 1958–1967 data.[2] These price deflators are used to deflate Becker's series on total utilized net material product in current prices to 1955 prices.[3] The result is given in column 1 of table 6–4.

Notes

1. Abraham S. Becker, "National Income Accounting in the U.S.S.R.," p. 95.
2. The equation is $P = 96.8 - 0.549(\text{year} - 1963)$. $R^2 = .86; DW = 1.86$; t ratio of (year − 1963) = 7.44.
3. Becker, "National Income Accounting," p. 97.

Appendix 6D

The values of the binary variable for weather are based on three U.S. government publications.[1] Diamond refers to 1958 and 1964 as "years of exceptionally favorable growing conditions" and 1956 and 1961 as "above average." He describes 1955, 1957, 1960, and 1962 as "more or less normal." These were given a value of 0. The year 1963 is described by Diamond as having "exceptionally poor growing conditions," and 1959 is described as having the "most unfavorable growing conditions" in the 1955–1959 period. These two years got a 1. Diamond and Krueger refer to the weather of 1965 (and 1963) as "disastrous." Thus 1965 was given a 1. The 1968 publication describes the weather of 1966 as "exceptionally favorable" and the weather of 1967 as "more normal." Therefore 1966 and 1967 received a 0.

Note

1. Douglas B. Diamond, "Trends in Output, Inputs, and Factor Productivity in Soviet Agriculture," p. 347; Joint Economic Committee, *Soviet Economic Performance,* p. 27; and Diamond and Constance B. Krueger, "Recent Developments in Output and Productivity in Soviet Agriculture," p. 317.

Appendix 6E

Nove describes a new (post-Stalin) lenient policy toward the private plots, for example, taxes were reduced, which was in effect before 1955.[1] However, an attack against the private plots, that is, a hostile policy, "seriously" got under way in 1958 and lasted throughout Khruschev's time in office.[2] After his fall, this policy was eased.[3] Thus the years 1955 to 1957 are given a 0, 1958 to 1964 a 1, and 1965 to 1967 a 0.

Notes

1. Alec Nove, *An Economic History of the U.S.S.R.,* p. 329.
2. Ibid., p. 366.
3. Keith Bush, "Agricultural Reforms since Khruschev," pp. 468-69.

Appendix 6F

A series on accumulation and other expenditures (that is, net increments in fixed and working capital) and a series on increments to fixed "productive" capital and working capital (a Soviet definition, this roughly excludes services and administration) are taken from Becker.[1] These are converted to 1955 rubles by using the price deflators from appendix 6C. In order to get the total capital stock in each year from these series, at least one observation of the total capital stock is needed. This is obtained for 1960, again expressed in 1955 rubles. Two concepts of the capital stock are used: total nonresidential fixed capital plus working capital, and total fixed capital plus working capital. Moorsteen and Powell's estimates of total nonresidential fixed capital stock and total fixed capital are used.[2] Their estimate of total working capital, that is, inventories and so on, is also used.[3]

The 1960 figure in column 1 of table 6–5 is obtained by adding Moorsteen and Powell's estimates of total nonresidential fixed capital and total working capital. By using Becker's series on increments to fixed productive capital and working capital (deflated), the rest of the years in column 1 are calculated. The 1960 figure in column 2 is obtained by adding Moorsteen and Powell's estimates of total fixed capital and total working capital. Then, using Becker's accumulation and other expenditures series, the other years are calculated.

Note that the calculations for column 1 involve different concepts of the relevant capital stock. Not all nonresidential capital is classified as productive. Thus adding (or subtracting) productive capital increments only to Moorsteen and Powell's nonresidential fixed capital stock of 1960 does not yield accurate estimates on nonresidential fixed capital in other years. However, the objective for using the two series of capital stock is to check the sensitivity of the estimated equations to different specifications of the capital stock. The figures in column 1, although just an approximation of another concept of the capital stock, would seem to be good enough for such a modest objective.

Notes

1. Abraham S. Becker, "National Income Accounting in the U.S.S.R.," p. 97. The specific columns used were 9 and 5 plus 8.
2. Richard Moorsteen and Raymond P. Powell, *Soviet Capital Stock 1928–1962,* p. 200.
3. Ibid., p. 131.

Appendix 6G

Table 6G-1
Official Soviet Retail Price Data

Year	*Official State Retail Price Indexes*		
	Overall	*Food*	*Nonfood*
1955	100.0	100.0	100.0
1956	100.0	101.4	99.3
1957	100.0	101.4	99.3
1958	102.2	105.7	99.3
1959	101.4	105.0	98.5
1960	100.7	104.3	97.0
1961	100.0	103.5	96.3
1962	101.4	106.4	96.3
1963	102.2	108.5	96.3
1964	102.2	107.8	95.5
1965	101.4	107.8	94.0
1966	100.7	107.1	92.5
1967	100.7	107.1	92.5

Sources: Computed from *Nar. Khoz. 1960*, p. 716; *1959*, p. 677; *1965*, p. 652; *1962*, p. 532; *1922–1972*, p. 409; *1963*, p. 539; *1967*, p. 739; *1968*, p. 639; *1969*, p. 625; *1970*, p. 601; *1972*, p. 602.

7

Empirical Results

Equations to Be Estimated

The analysis of chapter 4 produced the following equation system:

$$L^s = L^s(B^0, H_{-1}/P, W/P, P^B/P, P^A/P) \qquad (4.12)$$

$$A^d = A^d(B^0, H_{-1}/P, W/P, P^B/P, P^A/P) \qquad (4.13)$$

$$s^d = s^d(B^0, H_{-1}/P, W/P, P^B/P, P^A/P) \qquad (4.14)$$

$$A^s = A^s(B^0, H_{-1}/P, W/P, P^B/P, P^A/P, G, R) \qquad (4.15)$$

$$A^d = A^s \qquad (4.16)$$

$$L^d = L^d(W/P, Q^0, K^0) \qquad (4.17)$$

$$L^s = L^d \qquad (4.18)$$

$$P = \lambda_1 P^A + \lambda_2 P^B \qquad (4.19)$$

Equation (4.19) can be rearranged to be

$$\frac{P^B}{P} = \frac{1}{\lambda_2} - \frac{\lambda_1}{\lambda_2}\frac{P^A}{P}$$

and then used to eliminate P^B/P from equations (4.12) to (4.15), in order to avoid problems of perfect multicollinearity. Thus, the linear versions of equations (4.12) to (4.18) are, respectively [the α's are the intercepts and the β's the slope coefficients in the linear versions of equations (4.12) to (4.18)],

$$L^s = \alpha_1 + \beta_{14}/\lambda_2 + \beta_{11}B^0 + \beta_{12}(H_{-1}/P) + \beta_{13}(W/P)$$
$$+ (\beta_{15} - \beta_{14}\lambda_1/\lambda_2)(P^A/P) \qquad (7.1)$$

$$A^d = \alpha_2 + \beta_{24}/\lambda_2 + \beta_{21}B^0 + \beta_{22}(H_{-1}/P) + \beta_{23}(W/P)$$
$$+ (\beta_{25} - \beta_{24}\lambda_1/\lambda_2)(P^A/P) \qquad (7.2)$$

81

$$s^d = \alpha_3 + \beta_{34}/\lambda_2 + \beta_{31}B^0 + \beta_{32}(H_{-1}/P) + \beta_{33}(W/P)$$
$$+ (\beta_{35} - \beta_{34}\lambda_1/\lambda_2)(P^A/P) \tag{7.3}$$

$$A^s = \alpha_4 + \beta_{44}/\lambda_2 + \beta_{41}B^0 + \beta_{42}(H_{-1}/P) + \beta_{43}(W/P)$$
$$+ (\beta_{45} - \beta_{44}\lambda_1/\lambda_2)(P^A/P) + \beta_{46}G + \beta_{47}R \tag{7.4}$$

$$A^d = A^s \tag{7.5}$$

$$L^d = \alpha_5 + \beta_{53}(W/P) + \beta_{58}Q^0 + \beta_{59}K^0 \tag{7.6}$$

$$L^s = L^d \tag{7.7}$$

Counting excluded exogenous variables and included endogenous variables in each equation indicates that equations (7.1), (7.2), (7.3), and (7.6) are over-identified while equation (7.4) is unidentified.[1] Note that there is not enough information to estimate the constant terms (the α's) or the slope coefficients of either P^B/P or $P^A/P(\beta_{14}, \ldots, \beta_{44}, \beta_{15}, \ldots, \beta_{45})$.

The main method used in this book for estimating the L^s, A^d, and s^d equations is three-stage least squares (3SLS), although some ordinary least-squares (OLS) and two-stage least-squares (2SLS) results are also reported. Throughout, the unidentified A^s equation is omitted. In the first stage, the endogenous variables on the right-hand sides of L^s, A^d, s^d, and L^d are regressed on all the exogenous variables in the system: B^0, P^B, H_{-1}, G, R, Q^0, and K^0. These regressions yield instruments to be used in place of the endogenous right-hand variables in the second-stage regression estimates of L^s, A^d, s^d, and L^d. Then the error terms of the second-stage estimated equations are used to derive the third-stage estimates of L^s, A^d, s^d, and L^d by a generalized least-squares technique. Only the estimates of the first three of these equations are of interest to us, so the L^d estimates are not reported here.

Estimates

Tables 7-1 and 7-2 present 3SLS estimates of equations (7.1) to (7.3).[2] Table 7-1 uses the low estimate of P^B and its associated variables (that is, B^0 and P calculated with the use of the low estimate of P^B); table 7-2 uses the high estimate. Recall from the preceding section that there is not enough information to derive estimates of the constant term or the coefficients of P^B/P and P^A/P. The predictions from chapter 4 that can be tested empirically are presented in table 7-3.

Comparing the results presented in tables 7-1 and 7-2 with the predictions in table 7-3, one can see that all the predicted signs are correct and that all but one—$\delta A^d/\delta(W/P)$—are correct and have t ratios greater than 2. It is the presence

Table 7-1
Three-Stage Least-Squares Linear Estimates, Low P^B

Variable	L^s	A^d	s^d
Constant	.377959	190.939	−47.4140
	(17.166)	(12.404)	(2.456)
B^0	.00155341	−.899734	−.424641
	(7.732)	(6.468)	(2.292)
H_{-1}/P	−.000566027	.534027	−.264887
	(2.909)	(3.898)	(1.617)
W/P	.00166361	.364223	2.91192
	(2.610)	(0.822)	(5.053)
P^A/P	.000564284	−.445660	−.540664
	(2.880)	(3.236)	(3.248)
R^2	.997	.942	.901
DW	2.878	2.367	2.185

Note: Signed values are those of the slope coefficient. Figures in parentheses are absolute values of t ratios, that is, the ratio of the coefficient to the standard error. R^2 is 1 minus the ratio of the sum of squared residuals to the total sum of squares. DW is the Durbin-Watson statistic. In all cases, the sample size is 13.

Table 7-2
Three-Stage Least-Squares Linear Estimates, High P^B

Variable	L^s	A^d	s^d
Constant	.394840	182.961	−41.2168
	(25.286)	(12.512)	(2.158)
B^0	.00151320	−.908121	−.420540
	(9.869)	(6.345)	(2.158)
H_{-1}/P	−.000705391	.563762	−.251664
	(4.544)	(3.871)	(1.357)
W/P	.00244203	.247590	2.86018
	(4.810)	(0.521)	(4.536)
P^A/P	.0000555442	−.302335	−.584725
	(0.378)	(2.194)	(3.364)
R^2	.998	.942	.898
DW	2.496	2.252	2.249

of a quantity variable that distinguishes a disequilibrium demand function from the usual demand function. Hence the key statistic to examine is the coefficient of B^0 in each of the estimated equations. As has been seen, the signs of all these are correct and have t ratios exceeding 2. Direction of response is all that is formally predicted by the disequilibrium model, and so the conclusion of the empirical results presented here is that the model predicts very well.

Table 7-3
Predictions

Variable	L^s	A^d	s^d
B^0	+	−	−
H_{-1}/P	−	+	?
W/P	?	+	+

In order to test the robustness of the above conclusions, results using several different data and model specifications are presented in tables 7-4, 7-5, and 7-6. In the first two rows of the tables, the estimates from tables 7-1 and 7-2 are repeated for easy reference. In the next two rows, an alternative B^0 variable that incorporates personal services is used. The fifth row reflects the estimates obtained when official data for B^0, P^B, and P are used. In the sixth and seventh rows, an alternative L^s variable (annual average civilian employment) was used, and in the next two rows an alternative K^0 was used (nonresidential and working capital). In the tenth and eleventh rows an additional binary variable representing good weather was added to the A^s equation; and in the last two rows binary variables representing the relaxation of the labor laws in 1956 and the anticipation of the 1961 currency reform were added to the household sector's equations. (The labor-law change variable was added also to L^d.)

As indicated in the tables, the use of an alternative B^0 variable, an alternative K^0 variable, or the addition of a good weather binary variable does not affect anything of importance. The use of the official data (in the fifth row) reduces the t ratio of the coefficient of H_{-1}/P in the L^s equation to below 2, but the crucial B^0 coefficients in all three equations still have t ratios that exceed 2. In addition, the signs of the coefficients remain unchanged, although some of the point estimates of the coefficients differ noticeably in size (for example, those of B^0 in L^s and A^d).

The results reported in tables 7-1 and 7-2 use average nonprivate civilian employment as calculated in chapter 6 as the labor variable. This would seem to be a better choice than annual average civilian employment (also reported in chapter 6) because it allows the substitution of private production for official employment to show up as an increase in leisure (as discussed in chapter 4). The model was estimated using average civilian employment as L^s, and the results are presented in the sixth and seventh rows of tables 7-4, 7-5, and 7-6. The estimates of A^d and s^d equations are little affected, but there are some interesting changes in the L^s equation estimates. The t ratios of the coefficients of B^0 in the L^s equations are less than half those in tables 7-1 and 7-2, and the point estimates of the coefficients themselves are also less than half those in tables

7-1 and 7-2 (although the change in magnitude of the L^s variable explains some of the latter difference). These results constitute weak evidence that private production is an important way in which the Soviet household sector reacts to shortages on the official retail market, since the measure of labor supply that includes time spent in private production is less sensitive to changes in the quantity constraint than is a labor supply measure that excludes such time.

A household can manipulate its labor supply through participation or lack thereof of either spouse. Additionally, turnover and time spent between jobs can be increased or decreased. However, both options are reflected in the two L^s variables used here, although not as dramatically as they would be if presented on their own. Another alternative open to the worker wishing to decrease his labor supply and increase his consumption of leisure is the possibility of "on-the-job leisure," that is, less effort on the job. This type of decrease in labor supply would not be reflected in the labor supply variables used here.[3]

As mentioned in chapter 3, the change in the labor laws in 1956 may have influenced the household sector's behavior and labor demand of enterprises in 1956, and anticipation of the currency reform of 1961 may have influenced the household sector's behavior in 1960. In order to allow for these effects, two binary variables were constructed: LABLAW and CURREF. Their definitions as well as the estimates obtained using them are presented in tables 7-4, 7-5, and 7-6. In only one instance—LABLAW in L^s with low P^B—does a t ratio of a binary variable exceed 2. The other coefficients are not appreciably affected, although the coefficients of B^0 in s^d change noticeably and one of these has a t ratio just slightly below 2 (last row). Thus, it would appear that the binary variables are not needed except perhaps in the L^s equation. However, since even in this case the evidence is mixed, the present discussion focuses on the estimates presented in tables 7-1 and 7-2. Note, however, that the coefficient of LABLAW in the L^s equation is positive, which indicates that elimination of laws against labor mobility actually may have *increased* labor supply in 1956. Perhaps there is a lesson to be learned here.

Thus, the results presented in tables 7-4, 7-5, and 7-6 indicate that the conclusions as to the predictive power of the disequilibrium model are quite robust.

The Household Sector Response Pattern

Attention now turns to the relative size of the various responses of the household sector to changes in the quantity of goods available on the controlled market. In the general equation

$$y = \alpha + \beta_1 x_1 + \cdots + \beta_n x_n$$

Table 7-4
Alternative Specification[a] Three-Stage Least-Squares Estimates: L^s Equation

Case	Constant	B^0	H_{-1}/P	W/P	p^A/P	LABLAW	CURREF
1. Table 7-1 (reference case)	.378(17.166)	.00155(7.732)	-.000566(2.909)	.00166(2.610)	.000564(2.880)		
2. Table 7-2 (reference case)	.395(25.286)	.00151(9.869)	-.000705(4.544)	.00244(4.810)	.0000555(0.378)		
3. Alternative B^0, low BB	.394(18.745)	.00157(7.955)	-.000537(2.922)	.00143(2.283)	.000506(2.696)		
4. Alternative B^0, high pB	.407(27.256)	.00152(10.101)	-.000669(4.552)	.00217(4.350)	.0000515(0.368)		
5. Official B^0, pB, P	.409(15.022)	.00114(4.976)	-.000227(1.121)	.000784(1.026)	.00101(3.846)		
6. Alternative L^s, low pB	.507(26.497)	.000604(3.248)	-.000416(2.567)	.00357(6.203)	.000212(1.289)		
7. Alternative L^s, high pB	.516(32.528)	.000569(3.854)	-.000562(3.927)	.00434(9.018)	-.000209(1.552)		
8. Alternative K^0, low pB	.378(17.097)	.00156(7.735)	-.000568(2.873)	.00164(2.546)	.000556(2.764)		
9. Alternative K^0, high pB	.396(25.437)	.00151(9.874)	-.000703(4.509)	.00244(4.775)	.0000442(0.297)		
10. Including good weather, low pB	.378(17.122)	.00156(7.751)	-.000558(2.875)	.00161(2.558)	.000581(3.014)		

11. Including good weather, high P^B	.398(26.396)	.00153(10.304)	-.000664(4.453)	.00224(4.656)	.000104(0.740)		
12. Including shift variables, low P^B	.382(17.761)	.00175(8.357)	-.000569(3.390)	.00115(1.746)	.000579(3.444)	.00755(2.131)	-.0000304(0.009)
13. Including shift variables, high P^B	.390(24.337)	.00157(9.581)	-.000705(5.081)	.00230(4.176)	.000111(0.860)	.00357(1.311)	.00291(1.025)

Note: Signed values are those of the slope coefficient. Figures in parentheses are absolute value of t ratios, that is, the ratio of the coefficient to the standard error. In all cases, the sample size is 13.

[a]The alternative B^0 is constructed as follows: (1) the two P^B series in table 6–9 are rebased to 1968 using values taken from another study (D. Howard, "A Note on Hidden Inflation in the Soviet Union," p. 607)—110.1 for the low P^B series and 113.5 for the high P^B series; (2) the nominal retail sales series from table 6–2 is then converted to 1968 rubles by means of these P^B series and added to the data on personal services in 1968 rubles presented in the same table; (3) the resulting two series are then expressed as an index, divided by working-age population, and used as an alternative B^0 series.

The official data on B^0, P^B, and P are from tables 6–1 and 6–2.

The alternative L^s is average civilian employment from table 6–3.

The alternative K^0 is nonresidential and working capital from table 6–5.

The good-weather binary variable equals 1 in 1958, 1964, and 1966 and 0 in the other years.

The labor law binary variable (LABLAW) is 1 in 1956 and 0 elsewhere; the currency reform binary variable (CURREF) is 1 in 1960 and 0 elsewhere.

Table 7-5

Alternative Specification Three-Stage Least-Squares Estimates: A^d Equation

Case	Constant	B^0	H_{-1}/P	W/P	p^A/P	LABLAW	CURREF
1. Table 7-1 (reference case)	191.(12.404)	-.900(6.468)	.534(3.898)	.364(0.822)	-.446(3.236)		
2. Table 7-2 (reference case)	183.(12.512)	-.908(6.345)	.564(3.871)	.248(0.521)	-.302(2.194)		
3. Alternative B^0, low pB	182.(12.512)	-.909(6.839)	.518(4.002)	.504(1.183)	-.413(3.136)		
4. Alternative B^0, high pB	176.(12.721)	-.920(6.709)	.545(3.975)	.415(0.907)	-.300(2.294)		
5. Official B^0, pB, P	175.(13.045)	-.723(6.479)	.415(3.824)	.532(1.442)	-.503(3.887)		
6. Alternative L^s, low pB	188.(11.886)	-.875(6.212)	.506(3.569)	.385(0.854)	-.437(3.071)		
7. Alternative L^s, high pB	180.(12.101)	-.884(6.140)	.547(3.675)	.233(0.484)	-.277(1.967)		
8. Alternative K^0, low pB	191.(12.346)	-.893(6.398)	.529(3.810)	.363(0.812)	-.451(3.200)		
9. Alternative K^0, high pB	182.(12.313)	-.899(6.250)	.555(3.733)	.251(0.521)	-.298(2.093)		
10. Including good weather, low pB	191.(12.424)	-.898(6.457)	.538(3.955)	.345(0.789)	-.441(3.267)		
11. Including good weather, high pB	183.(12.628)	-.912(6.399)	.566(3.941)	.251(0.542)	-.302(2.225)		
12. Including shift variables, low pB	195.(10.867)	-.926(5.276)	.524(3.759)	.458(0.829)	-.498(3.562)	-2.16(0.722)	-2.54(0.866)
13. Including shift variables, high pB	187.(10.655)	-.915(5.010)	.548(3.633)	.311(0.513)	-.365(2.607)	-1.20(0.390)	-2.83(0.922)

Table 7-6
Alternative Specification Three-Stage Least-Squares Estimates: s^d Equation

Case	Constant	B^0	H_{-1}/P	W/P	p^A/P	LABLAW	CURREF
1. Table 7-1 (reference case)	-47.4(2.456)	-425(2.292)	-.265(1.617)	2.91(5.053)	-.541(3.248)		
2. Table 7-2 (reference case)	-41.2(2.158)	-421(2.158)	-.252(1.357)	2.86(4.536)	-.585(3.364)		
3. Alternative B^0, low p^B	-51.8(2.650)	-424(2.218)	-.275(1.666)	2.97(4.966)	-.525(3.104)		
4. Alternative B^0, high p^B	-45.0(2.298)	-414(2.035)	-.269(1.426)	2.93(4.435)	-.586(3.295)		
5. Official B^0, p^B, P	-52.2(2.532)	-457(2.627)	-.273(1.790)	3.04(5.261)	-.542(2.730)		
6. Alternative L^s, low p^B	-50.9(2.759)	-447(2.464)	-.312(2.017)	3.14(5.617)	-.591(3.742)		
7. Alternative L^s, high p^B	-41.9(2.264)	-429(2.229)	-.343(1.932)	3.21(5.214)	-.733(4.425)		
8. Alternative K^0, low p^B	-48.5(2.450)	-442(2.341)	-.255(1.475)	2.93(4.933)	-.522(2.970)		
9. Alternative K^0, high p^B	-40.1(2.041)	-436(2.209)	-.236(1.212)	2.85(4.390)	-.583(3.140)		
10. Including good weather, low p^B	-47.9(2.472)	-433(2.331)	-.278(1.707)	2.99(5.226)	-.563(3.441)		
11. Including good weather, high p^B	-42.6(2.237)	-422(2.163)	-.271(1.474)	2.93(4.738)	-.602(3.503)		
12. Including shift variables, low p^B	-55.8(2.325)	-529(2.131)	-.256(1.404)	3.18(4.140)	-.485(2.624)	-2.31(0.522)	3.64(0.955)
13. Including shift variables, high p^B	-48.2(1.999)	-512(1.981)	-.237(1.159)	3.06(3.629)	-.526(2.784)	-2.36(0.532)	3.16(0.762)

the elasticity[4] of response is defined as

$$\epsilon_{yi} = \frac{\beta_i x_i}{y}$$

This book uses the point estimates of the slope coefficients for β_i and the mean values of the x_i and y. Table 7-7 presents the calculated values of the elasticities.

One can call the elasticities with respect to B^0, that is, ϵ_{LB}, ϵ_{AB}, and ϵ_{sB}, "spillover coefficients" in that they express the degree of spillover into the other markets associated with a change in the quantity constraint. The sign and size of these spillover coefficients convey information about the household response pattern to changes in the quantity constraint.

Based on the relative sizes of ϵ_{LB}, ϵ_{AB}, and ϵ_{sB} in table 7-7, one can conclude that shortages or repressed inflation has less of an effect on labor supply, more of an effect on collective farm market demand, and a relatively large effect on saving.[5] Thus, in terms of the household response pattern to repressed inflation, the present estimates indicate that saving is probably the most responsive outlet for excess demand, and next is the collective farm market. This study makes it possible to measure (roughly) the relative size of the various outlets for repressed inflation. It can be seen that the labor supply response is not as large (in terms of percentage changes) as the other alternatives are.

The relatively small labor supply response is probably the result of the authorities' use of coercion. There are many coercive institutions in the Soviet labor market, for example, the antiparasite laws.[6] These exist probably for the express purpose of discouraging a large labor supply response, and in any case this is one of their effects. Of the other two spillover markets, the fact that saving seems to be more responsive than collective farm market demand may indicate that the Soviet consumer has hope for the future. Expectations about the availability of consumer goods in the future are probably the most important determinant of the relative sizes of these two responses. Such expectations may be influenced by government promises of future consumer goods as well as by actual production performance. Expectations are probably a determinant of the relatively small labor supply response as well.

Table 7-7
Elasticities of Response with Respect to B^0

Variable	L^s	A^d	s^d
B^0 (table 7-1 estimates)	.32	-1.47	-4.81
B^0 (table 7-2 estimates)	.30	-1.46	-4.77

Repressed Inflation in the Soviet Economy

Not much has been done in regard to studying inflationary pressures in the Soviet Union. The classic article is Holzman's 1960 piece.[7] Holzman places most of the blame for Soviet inflationary pressures on wage competition for labor, which bids wages up. This upward drift of wages is financed by loans to the enterprises by the central bank. Hence the authorities have no effective control on the growth of the money supply, which grows by way of wage overexpenditures. Most of this increase in the money supply goes into the "cash sector," that is, the household sector, and thus creates excess demand. According to Holzman, the process was slowed down by the introduction of controls on the mobility of labor in 1938.[8] Holzman also feels that laws about wage overexpenditures have solved the problem for the postwar period. However, Fearn has pointed out that these laws are easily circumvented, and wage overexpenditures again became a problem after 1953.[9]

Holzman views the collective farm market as the primary outlet for demand not satisfied on the state retail market. Thus the difference between the two sets of prices is an indicator of inflationary pressure. He presents two measures. One is simply the ratio between state prices and collective farm market prices. The second takes volume of sales into account. The second index indicates the excess money spent because of the higher prices on the collective farm market in relation to total sales valued at state prices. Holzman considers the second to be the better measure but recognizes its limitations by calling it a "partial indicator of suppressed inflation."[10]

Subsequent work has used either a variant of Holzman's measures or another indicator of suppressed inflation—trends in savings deposits. In their 1966 study, Bronson and Severin define inflationary pressure as "the excess monetary demand for consumer goods caused by a gap between the amount of money supplied to the economy and the amount actually needed to purchase current levels of output at planned prices."[11] They present two types of indicators of inflationary trends: the difference between state and collective farm market prices and trends in savings deposits. Two measures of the price differences are given. One is a simple ratio of free market food prices to state food prices, and the other is the second of Holzman's measures presented earlier.[12] They conclude that "although the indicators described above do not provide precise measures of the degree of repressed inflation both suggest that such pressures have grown in the past several years."[13]

In 1973, Bronson and Severin again stress the inadequacies of current measures of Soviet inflation:

> At best, the measurement of inflationary pressures in the U.S.S.R. is difficult because of the lack of comprehensive official data. . . . the ratio between prices in the CFM and state stores is the best available statistical measure of the state's failure to absorb excess purchasing power.[14]

They present these ratios and discuss them but point out that the diminishing importance of the collective farm market (in terms of its share of total retail sales) has "limited the usefulness of this indicator of inflationary pressure."[15] Bush uses the rise in savings as "the most dramatic indicator of repressed inflation" in the Soviet Union. He has also made an attempt to estimate household money incomes and outlays and thus the difference between "purchasing power and the value of desirable goods and services made available."[16]

Portes argues that although relative prices in the Soviet Union are incorrect, there is no significant overall repressed inflation.[17] Portes's argument raises an interesting question. However, for present purposes it makes no difference if Portes is correct or not. Incorrect relative prices also create disequilibria and spillover effects, and the disequilibrium model developed in this book is still relevant. (See the material on the n-good case in chapter 4.) In fact, a situation in which relative prices are set incorrectly might also be called repressed inflation, since certain prices are not allowed to rise to their market-clearing levels.

The analysis of this book generates some new information about past inflationary experience. The elasticities with respect to B^0 (that is, ϵ_{LB}, ϵ_{AB}, and ϵ_{sB}), here called spillover coefficients, convey information about the household's response pattern to repressed inflation. As can be seen from table 7-7, the Soviet household reacts to a change in the quantity constraint by changing its labor supply by a relatively small amount in the same direction, by changing its demand on the collective farm market to a relatively greater extent than its labor supply and in the opposite direction, and by changing its saving relatively more than its demand on the collective farm market and in the opposite direction of the change in the constraint. Note that it is the ordering of these responses which is of importance, not the exact numerical values of the elasticities. Thus saving is more sensitive than collective farm market demand to changes in quantity constraints and hence repressed inflation. Both are more sensitive than labor supply. Reasons for this particular response pattern as well as its implications are discussed in the next chapter.

This pattern would seem to fit the government's preferences rather well. The authorities, on practical grounds, want no decrease in labor supply. They oppose, mostly on ideological grounds, the role of the free markets, but on practical grounds they grudgingly allow some free markets. Finally, it would seem probable that the authorities would care little about the amount of saving except insofar as it indicates future problems.

Notes

1. The order condition for identification used in the text is necessary but not sufficient.

2. In the appendix to this chapter, 2SLS and OLS estimates of the equa-

tions are reported. As the reader can readily see, the estimates are quite similar to those discussed in the text.

3. At least in principle, this effect could be detected in labor productivity data.

4. An elasticity measure is used here rather than, say, marginal propensities because the data are not in comparable units (see chapter 6). Being unit-free, the elasticities are more easily interpreted than alternative measures.

5. In this study, the reaction to shortages per se is inferred from the household sector's reactions to changes in the quantities available of the goods in excess demand.

Construction of confidence intervals by the use of a twice-the-standard-error rule leads to the conclusion that in each row of table 7-7 the absolute size of ϵ_{LB} is significantly smaller than the absolute sizes of ϵ_{AB} and ϵ_{sB}. However, the sizes of ϵ_{AB} and ϵ_{sB} in each row are not significantly different from each other.

6. The antiparasite laws require that a person either have a job or be temporarily between jobs. See chapter 3 for a description of the major labor market institutions in the Soviet Union.

7. Franklyn D. Holzman, "Soviet Inflationary Pressures, 1928–1957."

8. Recall the discussion in chapter 5 of the implications for labor freedom when the government determines the society's output mix.

9. Robert M. Fearn, "Controls over Wage Funds and Inflationary Pressures in the U.S.S.R.," p. 191.

10. Holzman, "Soviet Inflationary Pressures," p. 168.

11. David W. Bronson and Barbara S. Severin, "Recent Trends in Consumption and Disposable Money Income in the U.S.S.R.," p. 513.

12. Ibid., pp. 514–15.

13. Ibid., p. 516.

14. Bronson and Severin, "Soviet Consumer Welfare: The Brezhnev Era," p. 381.

15. Ibid.

16. Keith Bush, "Soviet Inflation," pp. 100–101. It is interesting to note that Bush raises the question of the incentive effects of shortages, that is repressed inflation, on the labor supply, a question which is, of course, central to our study. See Bush, pp. 102–3.

17. Richard Portes, "Macroeconomic Equilibrium under Central Planning."

Appendix 7A

Table 7A-1
Two-Stage Least-Squares Linear Estimates, Low P^B

Variable	L^s	A^d	s^d
Constant	.366589	184.760	−29.6034
	(15.850)	(11.643)	(1.329)
B^0	.00161861	−.864274	−.526834
	(7.863)	(6.119)	(2.657)
H_{-1}/P	−.000668369	.478375	−.104507
	(3.212)	(3.351)	(0.522)
W/P	.00181648	.447322	2.67243
	(2.753)	(0.988)	(4.206)
P^A/P	.000570913	−.442081	−.551011
	(2.736)	(3.088)	(2.742)
R^2	.997	.945	.915
DW	3.016	2.343	2.489

Table 7A-2
Two-Stage Least-Squares Linear Estimates, High P^B

Variable	L^s	A^d	s^d
Constant	.387776	177.061	−24.8819
	(24.198)	(11.859)	(1.194)
B^0	.00156106	−.868157	−.531205
	(10.079)	(6.016)	(2.637)
H_{-1}/P	−.000772777	.507547	−.0959340
	(4.808)	(3.390)	(0.459)
W/P	.00252854	.319696	2.66032
	(4.882)	(0.663)	(3.950)
P^A/P	.0000587615	−.299572	−.592284
	(0.385)	(2.109)	(2.987)
R^2	.998	.945	.911
DW	2.640	2.230	2.512

Table 7A-3
Ordinary Least-Squares Linear Estimates, Low P^B

Variable	L^s	A^d	s^d
Constant	.370577	178.522	-22.5336
	(16.576)	(11.763)	(1.054)
B^0	.00163766	-.894054	-.489433
	(8.078)	(6.496)	(2.524)
H_{-1}/P	-.000673744	.454606	-.0711897
	(3.351)	(3.331)	(0.370)
W/P	.00178046	.618936	2.44372
	(2.923)	(1.497)	(4.194)
P^A/P	.000528752	-.429365	-.552367
	(2.769)	(3.312)	(3.024)
R^2	.997	.947	.917
DW	3.042	2.260	2.417

Table 7A-4
Ordinary Least-Squares Linear Estimates, High P^B

Variable	L^s	A^d	s^d
Constant	.394060	171.162	-18.4775
	(26.274)	(12.091)	(0.927)
B^0	.0016013	-.900788	-.496705
	(10.812)	(6.444)	(2.525)
H_{-1}/P	-.00713574	.468277	-.0546765
	(4.778)	(3.322)	(0.276)
W/P	.00219605	.556994	2.41055
	(4.814)	(1.294)	(3.978)
P^A/P	.000111536	-.318337	-.574849
	(0.822)	(2.485)	(3.189)
R^2	.998	.947	.913
DW	2.700	2.081	2.416

8 Conclusion

This book extends the formal analysis of macroeconomic disequilibrium and applies it to the Soviet economy. In this chapter, the theoretical and empirical conclusions are summarized, and policy implications are discussed.

Theoretical Conclusions

The distinctive feature of disequilibrium macroeconomic functions is the presence of quantity variables (as well as prices) as arguments, and the essential characteristic of a disequilibrium model is the explicit treatment of spillover effects. The model used in this book is a simple utility maximization model of household behavior where the possibility of quantity constraints is allowed. Using this, the rigorous choice-theoretic foundations of the Keynesian consumption function and disequilibrium theory in general can be established. The demand functions obtained have quantities as arguments, and spillover effects can be predicted. The model is general in that all, some, or none of the markets can clear. The functions implied, of course, depend on which markets are not clearing.

The present analysis provides the choice-theoretic basis of macroeconomic disequilibrium theory. This can be easily seen through use of a simple macroeconomic model of the household sector with three composite goods: consumption goods, saving, and leisure. Let C be consumption goods (real), S be saving (real), $T - L^s$ be leisure, L^s be labor supply, P^c be the price of C, P^s be the price of S, and W be the price of leisure (therefore, W is the wage rate). In the Keynesian case of unemployment disequilibrium, the macroeconomic functions are (assuming away aggregation problems)

$$C = C(L^{s0}, W, P^c, P^s) \quad \text{and} \quad S = S(L^{s0}, W, P^c, P^s)$$

or, in Keynes' terms,

$$C = C(L^{s0}) \quad \text{and} \quad S = S(L^{s0})$$

where the zero superscript indicates the quantity constraint in the labor market. The present analysis predicts

$$\frac{\delta C}{\delta L^{s0}} > 0 \quad \text{and} \quad \frac{\delta S}{\delta L^{s0}} > 0$$

(An increase in L^{s0} is a decrease in the constrained consumption of leisure; therefore the prediction is an increase in the demand for substitutes, that is, consumption goods and saving.)

In the case of unemployment, the consumer faces a budget constraint

$$WL^{s0} = P^c C + P^s S$$

If L^{s0} changes, then one or both of C and S also change in the same direction. This much follows from the budget constraint. However, the present analysis allows one to predict that both C and S will definitely change in the same direction if C, S, and leisure are all substitutes for one another. The present analysis provides the rigorous choice-theoretic foundations of Keynesian consumption theory and also shows that it depends on the (Hicks-Allen) substitutability of the composite goods involved as well as the existence of a constraint on labor supply. Keynesian consumption theory predicts that both C and S are increasing functions of income or labor supply. Thus something more than the budget constraint is needed. The present study provides this needed analysis.

In the case where there is excess demand for consumption goods, Barro and Grossman assert that "a household may react to frustrated commodity demand in two ways. First, the household may save the income which cannot be spent on consumption . . . second, the household may increase leisure by reducing its supply of labor."[1] This much follows from the constraint

$$WL^s = P^c C^0 + P^s S$$

However, their next statement, ". . . given that consumption, saving, and leisure in aggregate are substitutes, in general some combination of the two options will always be optimal,"[2] needs some demonstration which is not provided by Barro and Grossman. The present analysis demonstrates that the Barro and Grossman assertion is correct; and, in particular, it has shown that it really is optimal in that it is the result of utility-maximizing behavior, that is, the result of optimizing behavior. This can be seen as follows. For the excess-demand case, the functions are

$$L^s = L^s(C^0, W, P^c, P^s) \quad \text{and} \quad S = S(C^0, W, P^c, P^s)$$

and the analysis predicts

$$\frac{\delta L^s}{\delta C^0} > 0 \quad \text{and} \quad \frac{\delta S}{\delta C^0} < 0$$

which is what Barro and Grossman assert.[3]

So far we have assumed implicitly that price controls have been the cause of the quantity constraints faced by the consumer when he cannot purchase all that he would like at the prevailing prices. However, this assumption is not necessary for there to be quantity constraints and excess demand. If prices do not adjust instantaneously, then there can be a similar situation of excess demand and quantity constraints without price controls. Since one would not expect prices to adjust instantaneously,[4] the analysis in this book is fairly general. It seems that economies without perfectly flexible prices will be constantly subject to multiplier processes which amplify any excess-supply or excess-demand shock.[5] As Leijonhufvud puts it, "income-constrained processes result not only when price-level velocity is zero, but whenever it is short of infinite."[6] However, Leijonhufvud has had second thoughts. He contends that since real-world economies apparently are not as unstable as the original formulation of the disequilibrium model seems to imply, there must be something that dampens at least mild shocks. Leijonhufvud maintains that the holding of buffer stocks, particularly of money, will dampen those shocks that are within a certain range of seriousness (within the "corridor"). Outside this range, stocks are exhausted and the multiplier takes effect. The exhaustion of stocks is reinforced by revisions in expectations of, in the unemployment case, permanent income.[7] Grossman has replied that neither the size of stocks nor considerations of expected income have any qualitative significance on the disequilibrium model's original multiplier analysis.[8]

As shown in chapter 4, the inclusion of stocks of money has no effect on the qualitative predictions of the present analysis. Thus, even with stocks of money included in the analysis, the household sector's demand functions seem conducive to economic instability. Nevertheless, Leijonhufvud's point that real-world economies are not as unstable as the disequilibrium analysis would seem to imply appears to be well taken. The problem, however, lies not in the inclusion or exclusion of stocks, but in the interpretation of the constraints.

The concept of permanent income and consumption is useful here. For the unemployment case, Leijonhufvud states that the labor market constraint can be "of a magnitude and duration such that [the consumer] must revise downwards the subjective estimate of his permanent income."[9] This, in turn, will lead to a reduction in permanent consumption. Note that constraints of lesser magnitude and duration which do not affect the estimate of permanent income need not affect permanent consumption either since buffer stocks, accumulated for such occasions, can be drawn upon. In this way stocks are important to the analysis. Similarly for the excess-demand case, the consumer-goods market constraint can be such that the consumer must revise downward his estimate of permanent consumption. In terms of the analysis of chapter 4, define permanent consumption of the ith good to be $\bar{x}_i$. There will be an interval about $\bar{x}_i$ within which the consumer need not revise his estimate of permanent consumption of

x_i. This interval would correspond to what Leijonhufvud calls the corridor. Deviations in actual x_i consumption within this interval will not lead to spillover effects and multiplier processes. All this can be formalized as follows: Define the interval to be between x_i^L and x_i^u, where $x_i^L \leqslant \bar{x}_i \leqslant x_i^u$. Thus, if $b_i > x_i^L$ $(i \neq L)$ and $b_L < x_L^u$, there are no spillover effects (other than changes in buffer stocks) and hence no multiplier processes. If at least one of these conditions is violated, then an active quantity constraint is added to the consumer's maximization problem, and the analysis proceeds as in chapter 4.

This book has generalized some results of rationing theory and has analyzed quantity-constrained consumer behavior in general. Tobin's discussion of the incentive effects of rationing anticipated some of Barro and Grossman's work on the spillover effects of general excess demand, that is, decreases in labor supply and increases in saving. This book has rigorously derived these effects for the general disequilibrium case and has shown what conditions are necessary for them to strictly hold (quantity constraints and substitutability).

The analysis of this book has developed the choice-theoretic foundations of the Barro and Grossman disequilibrium model. In the process it has been found that the Keynesian consumption function's well-known properties depend on a constrained labor supply and substitutability among consumption goods, saving, and leisure. The former condition must hold in order for employment or labor income to enter the function. In the absence of a labor supply constraint, labor income is a choice variable and therefore would not enter as an independent variable. The substitutability ensures predictions consistent with those of Keynes.

Empirical Conclusions

Two major conclusions can be drawn from the empirical work in this book. First, the empirical work is a test of the disequilibrium model's predictive ability, and the conclusion is that the model performs very well.

The second conclusion concerns the Soviet household response pattern to repressed inflation. The elasticities with respect to B^0 express the degree of spillover into other markets associated with a change in the quantity constraint. The sign and relative size of these elasticities convey information about the household response pattern to changes in the quantity constraint and repressed inflation in general. By comparing the relative sizes of these spillover coefficients, one can conclude that shortages or repressed inflation has relatively less of an effect on labor supply, more of an effect on collective farm market demand, and still more of an effect on saving. That is, in terms of the household response pattern to repressed inflation, saving is the most responsive outlet for excess demand and labor supply is the least.

Policy Implications

Disequilibrium prices have been a recurring phenomenon in the Soviet Union. Therefore, it is important to know their implications for economic performance and policy. Based on the household response pattern estimated here, whatever benefits the Soviet Union or its government gets from repressing inflation on the major consumer-goods market are obtained at relatively little present cost in that labor supply is less responsive to repressed inflation than are the demands for collective farm market goods and saving. However, saving may indicate future problems.

As mentioned in chapter 6, the relatively small labor supply response is probably the result of the authorities' use of coercion. As was seen in chapter 3, there are many coercive institutions in the Soviet labor market.[10] Of the other two spillover markets, the fact that saving is more responsive than collective farm market demand seems to indicate that the Soviet consumer has some hope for the future availability of consumption goods.

The disequilibrium model predicts that repressed inflation will have certain spillover effects. The policies that would bring about a desirable (from the authorities' point of view) response pattern are labor coercion and promises of more goods in the future. (The latter encourage saving not only as an alternative to leisure, but also as an alternative to collective farm market demand.) The Soviet authorities apparently have used various policy measures, for example, labor coercion and promises about the future, to minimize the size of the most undesirable of these spillover effects (labor supply) and to maximize that of the least undesirable (saving).

Notes

1. Robert J. Barro and Herschel I. Grossman, "A General Disequilibrium Model of Income and Employment," p. 91.

2. Ibid.

3. The functions used here are not exactly those proposed by Barro and Grossman. Their functions include the real amount of savings carried over from the previous period as an argument. Inclusion of savings has no effect on the analysis (see chapter 4). Using a much different theoretical framework, Dean S. Dutton and William P. Gramm, "Transactions Costs, the Wage Rate, and the Demand for Money," have derived the Barro and Grossman results for the excess-demand case.

4. See, for example, Axel Leijonhufvud, *On Keynesian Economics and the Economics of Keynes*, p. 69.

5. See, for example, Barro and Grossman, "Suppressed Inflation and the Supply Multiplier."

6. Leijonhufvud, *On Keynesian Economics,* p. 67.

7. Leijonhufvud, "Effective Demand Failures," pp. 36–39, 41–43.

8. Grossman, "Effective Demand Failures: A Comment," p. 360, note 1.

9. Leijonhufvud, "Effective Demand Failures," p. 43.

10. An interesting historical example of the connection between coercion and the supply effects of shortages may very well be the period of the New Economic Policy (NEP). It might be argued that during this period, consumer-goods shortages reduced peasant grain supply and helped to bring on such coercive measures as first the forcible collections of grain and then the forcible collectivization of the peasants.

Bibliography

Alchian, Armen A. "Information Costs, Pricing, and Resource Unemployment." In *Microeconomic Foundations of Employment and Inflation Theory,* Edmund S. Phelps et al. New York: W.W. Norton & Company, 1970.

Barro, Robert J., and Grossman, Herschel I. "A General Disequilibrium Model of Income and Employment." *American Economic Review* 61 (March 1971): 82-93.

___ and ___. "Suppressed Inflation and the Supply Multiplier." *Review of Economic Studies* 41 (January 1974): 87-104.

___ and ___. *Money, Employment and Inflation.* New York: Cambridge University Press, 1976.

Becker, Abraham S. "National Income Accounting in the U.S.S.R." In *Soviet Economic Statistics,* edited by Vladimir G. Treml and John P. Hardt. Durham, N.C.: Duke University Press, 1972.

Bornstein, Morris. "Soviet Price Statistics." In *Soviet Economic Statistics,* edited by Vladimir G. Treml and John P. Hardt. Durham, N.C.: Duke University Press, 1972.

Boulding, Kenneth. "A Note on the Theory of the Black Market." *Canadian Journal of Economics and Political Science* 13 (February 1947): 115-18.

Bronson, David W., and Krueger, Constance B. "The Revolution in Soviet Farm Household Income, 1953-1967." In *The Soviet Rural Community,* edited by James R. Millar. Urbana: University of Illinois Press, 1971.

___, and Severin, Barbara S. "Recent Trends in Consumption and Disposable Money Income in the U.S.S.R." In *New Directions in the Soviet Economy.* Joint Economic Committee. Washington: Government Printing Office, 1966.

___ and ___. "Soviet Consumer Welfare: The Brezhnev Era." In *Soviet Economic Prospects for the Seventies.* Joint Economic Committee. Washington: Government Printing Office, 1973.

Brown, Emily Clark. *Soviet Trade Unions and Labor Relations.* Cambridge, Mass.: Harvard University Press, 1966.

Bush, Keith. "Agricultural Reforms since Khrushchev." In *New Directions in the Soviet Economy.* Joint Economic Committee. Washington: Government Printing Office, 1966.

___. "Soviet Inflation." In *Banking, Money and Credit in Eastern Europe,* edited by M. Yves Laulan. NATO, 1973.

Central Intelligence Agency. "A Comparison of Consumption in the U.S.S.R. and the U.S." 1964.

Chapman, Janet G. *Real Wages in Soviet Russia since 1928.* Cambridge, Mass.: Harvard University Press, 1963.

Clower, Robert. "Keynes and the Classics: A Dynamical Perspective." *Quarterly Journal of Economics* 74 (May 1960): 318-23.

____. "The Keynesian Counterrevolution: A Theoretical Appraisal." In *The Theory of Interest Rates,* edited by F.H. Hahn and F.P.R. Brechling. London: Macmillan, 1965.

Diamond, Douglas B. "Trends in Output, Inputs, and Factor Productivity in Soviet Agriculture." In *New Directions in the Soviet Economy.* Joint Economic Committee. Washington: Government Printing Office, 1966.

____, and Krueger, Constance B. "Recent Developments in Output and Productivity in Soviet Agriculture." In *Soviet Economic Prospects for the Seventies.* Joint Economic Committee. Washington: Government Printing Office, 1973.

Dodge, Norton T., and Wilber, Charles K. "The Relevance of Soviet Industrial Experience for Less Developed Economies." *Soviet Studies* 21 (January 1970): 330–49.

Domar, Evsey D. "The Causes of Slavery or Serfdom: A Hypothesis." *Journal of Economic History* 30 (March 1970): 18–32.

Dutton, Dean S., and Gramm, William P. "Transactions Costs, the Wage Rate, and the Demand for Money." *American Economic Review* 63 (September 1973): 652–65.

Ellison, Herbert J. "Commentary." In *Soviet Agricultural and Peasant Affairs,* edited by Roy D. Laird. Lawrence: University of Kansas Press, 1963.

Fearn, Robert M. "Controls over Wage Funds and Inflationary Pressures in the U.S.S.R." *Industrial and Labor Relations Review* 18 (January 1965): 186–95.

Feshbach, Murray. "Manpower in the U.S.S.R.: A Survey of Recent Trends and Prospects." In *New Directions in the Soviet Economy.* Joint Economic Committee. Washington: Government Printing Office, 1966.

____, and Rapawy, Stephen. "Labor Constraints in the Five-Year Plan." In *Soviet Economic Prospects for the Seventies.* Joint Economic Committee. Washington: Government Printing Office, 1973.

Friedman, Milton. *Capitalism and Freedom.* Chicago: University of Chicago Press, 1962.

Gallik, David; Jesina, Cestmir; and Rapawy, Stephen. *The Soviet Financial System: Structure, Operation, and Statistics.* Washington: Bureau of the Census, 1968.

Garvy, George. *Money, Banking, and Credit in Eastern Europe.* New York: Federal Reserve Bank of New York, 1966.

Goldman, Marshall I. *Soviet Marketing.* New York: Free Press of Glencoe, 1963.

____. "Consumption Statistics." In *Soviet Economic Statistics,* edited by Vladimir G. Treml and John P. Hardt. Durham, N.C.: Duke University Press, 1972.

Green, H.A. John. *Aggregation in Economic Analysis: An Introductory Survey.* Princeton, N.J.: Princeton University Press, 1964.

Grossman, Herschel I. "Theories of Markets without Recontracting." *Journal of Economic Theory* 1 (December 1969): 476–79.

———. "Money, Interest, and Prices in Market Disequilibrium." *Journal of Political Economy* 79 (September/October 1971): 943-61.

———. "Was Keynes a 'Keynesian'? A Review Article." *Journal of Economic Literature* 10 (March 1972): 26-30.

———. "Effective Demand Failures: A Comment." *Swedish Journal of Economics* 76 (September 1974): 358-65.

Hanson, Philip. *The Consumer in the Soviet Economy.* Evanston, Ill.: Northwestern University Press, 1968.

Hayek, Friedrich A. *The Road to Serfdom.* Chicago: University of Chicago Press, 1944.

———. *The Constitution of Liberty.* Chicago: University of Chicago Press, 1960.

Holzman, Franklyn D. "Soviet Inflationary Pressures, 1928-1957: Causes and Cures." *Quarterly Journal of Economics* 74 (May 1960): 167-88.

Howard, David H. "A Note on Hidden Inflation in the Soviet Union." *Soviet Studies* 28 (October 1976): 599-608.

———. "The Disequilibrium Model in a Controlled Economy: An Empirical Test of the Barro-Grossman Model." *American Economic Review* 66 (December 1976): 871-79.

———. "Rationing, Quantity Constraints, and Consumption Theory." *Econometrica* 45 (March 1977): 399-412.

Joint Economic Committee. *Soviet Economic Performance.* Washington: Government Printing Office, 1968.

Karcz, Jerzy. "Quantitative Analysis of the Collective Farm Market." *American Economic Review* 54 (June 1964): 315-34.

———. "Seven Years on the Farm: Retrospect and Prospects." In *New Directions in the Soviet Economy.* Joint Economic Committee. Washington: Government Printing Office, 1966.

Keynes, John Maynard. *The General Theory of Employment, Interest, and Money.* New York: Harcourt, Brace and Company, 1936.

———. "The General Theory of Employment." *Quarterly Journal of Economics* 51 (February 1937): 209-23.

Laird, Roy D. "The Politics of Soviet Agriculture." In *Soviet Agricultural and Peasant Affairs,* edited by Roy D. Laird. Lawrence: University of Kansas Press, 1963.

Leedy, Frederick A. "Demographic Trends in the U.S.S.R." In *Soviet Economic Prospects for the Seventies.* Joint Economic Committee. Washington: Government Printing Office, 1973.

Leijonhufvud, Axel. *On Keynesian Economics and the Economics of Keynes.* New York: Oxford University Press, 1968.

———. *Keynes and the Classics.* London: Institute of Economic Affairs, 1969.

———. "Effective Demand Failures." *Swedish Journal of Economics* 75 (March 1973): 27-48.

Levine, Herbert S. "Pressure and Planning in the Soviet Economy." In *Indus-*

trialization in Two Systems: Essays in Honor of Alexander Gerschenkron, edited by Henry Rosovsky. New York: Wiley, 1966.

Miller, Margaret. *Rise of the Russian Consumer.* London: Institute of Economic Affairs, 1965.

Moorsteen, Richard, and Powell, Raymond P. *The Soviet Capital Stock, 1928–1962.* Homewood, Ill.: Richard D. Irwin, 1966.

Nash, Edmund. "Recent Changes in Labor Controls in the Soviet Union." In *New Directions in the Soviet Economy.* Joint Economic Committee. Washington: Government Printing Office, 1966.

Nove, Alec. *An Economic History of the U.S.S.R.* Baltimore, Md.: Penguin Books, 1969.

_____. *The Soviet Economy,* 2d rev. ed. New York: Frederick A. Praeger, 1969.

Patinkin, Don. "Involuntary Unemployment and the Keynesian Supply Function." *Economic Journal* 59 (September 1949): 360–83.

_____. *Money, Interest, and Prices,* 2d ed. New York: Harper & Row, 1965.

Pollak, Robert A. "Conditional Demand Functions and Consumption Theory." *Quarterly Journal of Economics* 83 (February 1969): 60–78.

Portes, Richard. "Macroeconomic Equilibrium under Central Planning." Institute for International Economic Studies, Seminar Paper No. 40, Stockholm, September 1974.

Powell, Raymond P. "Monetary Statistics." In *Soviet Economic Statistics,* edited by Vladimir G. Treml and John P. Hardt. Durham, N.C.: Duke University Press, 1972.

Schroeder, Gertrude E. "Labor Planning in the U.S.S.R." *Southern Economic Journal* 32 (July 1965): 63–72.

_____. "An Appraisal of Soviet Wage and Income Statistics." In *Soviet Economic Statistics,* edited by Vladimir G. Treml and John P. Hardt. Durham, N.C.: Duke University Press, 1972.

_____. "Consumer Problems and Prospects." *Problems of Communism* 22 (March-April 1973): 10–24.

Sherman, Roger, and Willett, Thomas D. "The Standardized Work Week and the Allocation of Time." *Kyklos* 25 (1972): 65–82.

Symons, Leslie. *Russian Agriculture.* London: G. Bell and Sons, 1972.

Tobin, James. "A Survey of the Theory of Rationing." *Econometrica* 20 (October 1952): 521–53.

_____, and Houthakker, H.S. "The Effects of Rationing on Demand Elasticities." *Review of Economic Studies* 18 (1950–1951): 140–53.

Ts. S.U. *Narodnoe Khoziaistvo SSSR v 1956 g.* Moscow, 1957.

_____. *Narodnoe Khoziaistvo SSSR v 1959 g.* Moscow, 1960.

_____. *Narodnoe Khoziaistvo SSSR v 1960 g.* Moscow, 1961.

_____. *Narodnoe Khoziaistvo SSSR v 1961 g.* Moscow, 1962.

_____. *Narodnoe Khoziaistvo SSSR v 1962 g.* Moscow, 1963.

_____. *Narodnoe Khoziaistvo SSSR v 1963 g.* Moscow, 1964.

_____. *Narodnoe Khoziaistvo SSSR v 1964 g.* Moscow, 1965.

_____. *Narodnoe Khoziaistvo SSSR v 1965 g.* Moscow, 1966.

_____. *Narodnoe Khoziaistvo SSSR v 1967 g.* Moscow, 1968.

_____. *Narodnoe Khoziaistvo SSSR v 1968 g.* Moscow, 1969.

_____. *Narodnoe Khoziaistvo SSSR 1922-1972 gg.* Moscow, 1972.

_____. *Trud v SSSR.* Moscow, 1968.

Tucker, Donald P. "Macroeconomic Models and the Demand for Money under Market Disequilibrium." *Journal of Money, Credit, and Banking* 3 (February 1971): 57-83.

_____. "Patinkin's Macro Model as a Model of Market Disequilibrium." *Southern Economic Journal* 39 (October 1972): 187-203.

Yeager, Leland B. "The Keynesian Diversion." *Western Economic Journal* 11 (June 1973): 150-63.

Index

Index

About the Author

David H. Howard is an economist in the International Finance Division of the Board of Governors of the Federal Reserve System. He received the B.A. in economics from Hamilton College in 1968 and the Ph.D. from the University of Virginia in 1975.